Dream State

To the memory of my parents –
Daniel and Hester.

Dream State

The New Scottish Poets

Edited by Daniel O'Rourke

Polygon, Edinburgh

Selection © Polygon 1994

Introduction © Daniel O'Rourke 1994

© Copyright of poems resides with the individual poets;
the acknowledgements on pp. 234–35 constitute an extension
of this copyright page.

Published by
Polygon
22 George Square
EDINBURGH

Set in Sabon by ROM-Data Ltd, Falmouth, Cornwall
and printed and bound in Great Britain by Page Bros Limited, Norwich,
Norfolk

ISBN 0 7486 6169 7

The Publisher acknowledges subsidy from the Scottish Arts
Council towards the publication of this volume.

The Publisher acknowledges an award from the Deric Bolton
Poetry Trust towards the publication of this volume.

Foreword

The poets gathered in *Dream State* are all under forty. Each has published at least one book, or won an Eric Gregory Award, (recognition of a collection-in-waiting). Since Scotland's many literary magazines are themselves sizeable, the stipulation of a volume, no matter how slim, seemed like the only way of slipping a chock under Sisyphus' boulder. To give those chosen some hope of establishing a rapport with the reader, I have opted for more poems by fewer poets. Each poet was then given the opportunity to provide a statement about his or her work.

Taste, naturally, enters into this selection but not, I hope, caprice. Good writers from elsewhere who have chosen to live in Scotland were omitted not because they aren't Scottish, but because their poems didn't seem to be. My thanks to all the poets whose work I had the pleasure of reading, whether included here or not. Many people helped me turn *Dream State* into reality. They know who they are. And how grateful I am.

There is no passport to this country,
It exists as a quality of the language.
'Dingle Dell' by W.N. Herbert

Contents

Carol Ann Duffy (b. 1955)

John Burnside (b. 1955)

Peter McCarey (b. 1956)

Alan Riach (b. 1957)

Elizabeth Burns (b. 1957)

William Hershaw (b. 1957)

Robert Alan Jamieson (b. 1958)

Robert Crawford (b. 1959)

David Kinloch (b. 1959)

Meg Bateman (b. 1959)

Iain Bamforth (b. 1959)

Graham Fulton (b. 1959)

Daniel O'Rourke (b. 1959)

Maud Sulter (b. 1960)

Jackie Kay (b. 1961)

W.N. Herbert (b. 1961)

Kathleen Jamie (b. 1962)

Don Paterson (b. 1963)

Raymond Friel (b. 1963)

Angela McSeveney (b. 1964)

Alison Kermack (b. 1965)

Richard Price (b. 1966)

Roddy Lumsden (b. 1966)

Stuart A. Paterson (b. 1966)

Anne C. Frater (b. 1967)

Introduction
Daniel O'Rourke

Dream State presents the work of a new generation of Scottish poets. Since Scottish culture (like this anthology) has the advantage of Scots and Gaelic, two distinct and thriving poetic tongues, Scotland's newest poetry is especially rich.

In addition, these writings serve as bulletins from, and memorials to, a transforming stretch of a small country's history. A substantial number of the poems are about the state of Scotland, both actual and envisioned; yet there is nothing narrowly chauvinistic about them.

If Pound was right and poetry really is 'news that stays news', much of the verse gathered in the book has nothing to fear from the long run. As usual, Edwin Morgan puts it very well:

'Normally it ought to be enough to be called a poet, *tout court*, but I feel the present moment of Scottish history very strongly and want to acknowledge it, despite the fact that my interests extend to languages, genres, and disciplines outwith Scotland or its traditions. Much modern Scottish poetry differs from poetry in the rest of the British isles by being written in Gaelic or in some form of Scots, but my point would be even if it were written in English it may be part of a hardly definable intention in the author to help build up the image of poetry which his country presents to the world. If Scotland became independent tomorrow, there is no guarantee that it would enter a golden age of literary expression. Yet I am sure I am not mistaken in sensing, even among those who are less than sympathetic to devolutionary or wider political change, an awareness of such change which in subtle ways affects creative endeavour, suggests a gathering of forces, a desire to "show" what can be done. The "Scottishness" may be no more than a writer deciding to remain and work in Scotland, though wooed elsewhere; and despite my phrase "no more than" I regard this as being important. More and more writers now take this decision. The result will be, I hope, that dedication to the art of

writing will not be unaccompanied by the other dedication – to a
society, to a place, to a nation – which can and will run the whole
gamut from the rabid to the near-invisible.'

That is the gamut this book hopes to run and I make no apology
for quoting Morgan at length, because his influence on Scotland's
younger poets has been enormous. In the verve and variety of his
verse, the insight and generosity of his teaching and in the copious
modernity of his imagination, Morgan is very much this
anthology's presiding spirit. Writing in 1979 in the magazine
Aquarius, he was responding to the coming to power of the
Thatcher government and Scotland's powerlessness after a ran-
corously-contested, listlessly-enacted referendum had failed to
secure even limited self-government.

Most of the writers in this book felt a similar need to 'acknowl-
edge the moment.' For some, the Thatcher election was the first
in which they had been eligible to vote. Our inability as a nation
to opt in sufficient numbers for the constitutional expression of
what had long been culturally obvious, did not for the most part
propel young writers into political activity. Disillusionment with
party politics tended to find expression in cultural commitment.
Of course, some explicitly political poetry was written then, and
since. And yet a kind of queasy quietism does seem to have
prevailed as far as day-to-day dialectics were concerned. The 80s
saw poem after poem present and represent this new Scotland.
Or (more exactly) *Scotlands*. For the poetry was characterised by
a vigorous pluralism as ideas and ideals of nation and nationhood
were explored, and Scots and Gaelic took on a new impetus. Not
just, or even first, in poetry. In pop and in painting. In classical
music. In design. In prose. In the media. An unprecedented
cultural confidence – and a *popular* cultural confidence at that –
offset the torpor and timidity of the politics of the decade. Often
it seemed that the poets, more confidently than the politicians,
were dreaming a new state.

At a time when the map of Europe, after various velvet revo-
lutions, is once again being bloodily redrawn, one would want to
be careful about the title *Dream State*. Used here (and borrowed
from a Stuart Paterson poem) the phrase should imply no narrow
nationalism. As Alasdair Gray points out in his polemic *Why
Scots Should Rule Scotland* 'the first people in Scotland to call

themselves Scots, were immigrants,' and 'Wee Scotlanders' have played no part in this cultural renaissance: a Scot leaving Scotland remains one, anyone coming to live here *becomes* one. But at the same time as some writers have moved away, poets such as Robert Crawford, David Kinloch and Iain Bamforth have returned to Scotland, fulfilling Morgan's hopes for 'a society, a place, a nation', and using history to help revive and revivify the spirit and matter of Scotland.

> . . . I came back here to choose my union
> On the side of the ayes, remaining a part
>
> Of this diverse assembly – Benbecula, Glasgow, Bow of
> Fife
> Voting with my feet, and this hand.
>
> 'A Scottish Assembly'

A forthright, fervent but questioning and complexly modern Scottishness informs much of the new Scottish poetry. By craftily and confidently entitling his poem (and indeed the collection it comes from) 'A Scottish Assembly', Robert Crawford thrusts poetry into the vacuum created by the lack of a legislative forum. Of course poetry *isn't* a substitute Shelleyian parliament and Crawford is kidding no one, himself least of all. But poetry can help focus and foment feeling that has no parliamentary outlet. The Scotland that Crawford speaks from and to (and therefore occasionally for) is a more self-assured and cheerful place, for all its recent social and economic travails than the country on whose behalf MacDiarmid picked up his moral megaphone in the 20s.

> A Scottish poet maun assume
> The burden o' his people's doom
> And dee to brak' their livin' tomb.
>
> (*A Drunk Man Looks At The Thistle*)

Just as Edwin Morgan (born in 1920) followed MacDiarmid's lead in dreaming up Scotlands – some of them even science fictional – so poets born in the 50s and 60s have joined Morgan in envisioning their own, other, better, Scotlands.

Of course, not all writers are equipped, or minded to accept such responsibilities, and lyric poetry in particular has always had a predisposition towards the personal and private. Of the writers assembled here, John Burnside, Meg Bateman, Angela McSeveney and Elizabeth Burns write an inward poetry, though a poetry that is never complacently solipsistic. More outgoing poets have their meditative moments too, *their* dream states. It isn't only in poetry that the last fifteen years or so have seen many people retreating from the crassness and craziness of much contemporary life. Their reveries are here too. As the folk singer Phil Ochs pointed out, 'in such an ugly time beauty is the true protest.'

In hoping for a poetic 'gathering of forces' Edwin Morgan expected no specific political allegiance and imposed no residency clause. Economic or emotional imperatives have kept a good number of young Scots poets furth of Scotland. That is the case with the sharply contrasting poets Carol Ann Duffy and John Burnside, each of whom left Scotland as a child and so can be said to have had little choice in the matter. Both were born in 1955 and are included in Douglas Dunn's *Faber Book of Twentieth Century Scottish Poetry* as well as in Bloodaxe's *The New Poetry*. They are this anthology's senior representatives and its starting point. Although neither has lived here for more than twenty years, the leaving of Scotland is a recurring theme in their work. As highly successful, complexly Scottish poets, writing at two kinds of remove from Scotland, Duffy and Burnside, both still comfortably under forty, establish a useful perspective. They represent a break between the established Scottish-domiciled poets who were born around 1950 – Ron Butlin, Andrew Greig, Frank Kuppner, Brian McCabe, and Tom Pow – and the poets born at the end of the decade, such as Peter McCarey, Alan Riach, Elizabeth Burns, David Kinloch, Graham Fulton and Robert Crawford.

Together, Duffy and Burnside have enjoyed considerable success issuing outstanding books from Anvil and Secker respectively. They may have left Scotland as children but Scotland, clinging tenaciously as ever, has not left them. Although they have made it clear in separate interviews that neither is comfortable being regarded as an exile, ('I just don't live there anymore', as Burnside put it) both have written poems of displacement centred on their country of birth.

Carol Ann Duffy's family moved from Glasgow to Stafford when she was just four. Her poem 'Originally', takes André Breton's conviction that 'childhood is the only reality' and twists and deepens it. In Duffy's poem 'All childhood is an emigration'. The wee girl's cry, 'I want our own country', is one that echoes far beyond one uprooted childhood in the Potteries. In another poem, the Scottish phrase, 'what like is it' (for 'what's it like') triggers nostalgia for mother and motherland both:

> I am homesick, free, in love
> with the way my mother speaks.
> > 'The Way My Mother Speaks'

The way Carol Ann Duffy speaks, whether in her monologues, in her love lyrics, or in her observational pieces, reveals one of the most supple and compelling voices in the poetry of the Dis-United Kingdom; one that sounds something like a more astringent and sardonic version of her friend Liz Lochhead's. 'Translating the English', something Carol Ann Duffy has been forced to do since primary school, introduces us to a wink-wink wideboy, doing a spot of back-of-a-lorry freelancing in the Heritage Industry. He'll sell the tourists anything. Or almost anything.

> You will be knowing of Charles Dickens and Terry Wogan
> and Scotland. All this can be arranged for cash no questions.
> Ireland not on.

In our Banana Monarchy, Scotland too, is seldom 'on'. Duffy's verse is a surveillance camera trained on the greedy and the seedy. She misses nothing except the distant decencies of the recent past.

No one has better caught the vicious vacuousness of England in the 80s. In another virtuoso (and Morganesque) monologue, a *Sun* headline writer boasts oafishly of his masterpiece; the poem is called 'Poet for our Times'. And that's precisely and eloquently what its creator is too. Duffy, for all her sometimes erotic and intimate lyricism, also writes outspoken poems about the condition of the state.

John Burnside, by contrast, is a poet of eternity, of dream. Although his break with Catholicism is less vituperative and final than Duffy's, it is a sufficiently marked severance to prevent him being considered as a conventional Catholic poet. His even-tempered, exquisitely-worked poems burn with a steady votive glow. Their externally focused, yet profoundly inward intensity gives Burnside's poems a vigil-like watchfulness; a meditational calm. Yet Scotland nags away at him too. 'Dundee' begins:

> The streets are waiting for a snow
> that never falls:
> too close to the water,
> too muffled in the afterwarmth of jute

This is the weather forecast by T.S. Eliot. But even without the snowfall of grace, redemption is possible for: 'the one who stands here proven after all'. It is not, I think, co-incidental that this 'proving' occurs in Scotland, or for that matter Dundee: the city of *Discovery*, and self-discovery, features prominently in this anthology.

Given John Burnside's underplaying of the notion of exile, a poem entitled 'Exile's Return' might be suspected of irony. It seems guilty only of ambivalence about an 'identity/to be assumed like tartan.' To ask 'Do we know/where we are in these tourist hills?' is to seek bearings that are at least partly spiritual. Burnside, whose father left Cowdenbeath for Corby in the early 60s has a poem called 'Flitting', whose very title exposes differences between Burnside's two cultures and their languages. His flitting one suspects was very much a removal, a dislocation that draws him back in search of solace. Yet the past and its comforts cannot always be relied upon:

> Memory, you should have known,
> is a double agent:
>
> one of those gaberdine
> people in films, a smiling
>
> Harry Lime.
>   'Anamnesis'

Burnside has spoken of his fascination with Orson Welles. (Author of *F for Fake*, and, in *The Third Man*, the embodiment of

the deceitful double agent.) But if his poems go to a film occasion-
ally, they never lose themselves in it. The cinema is just another
means of investigating the gap and overlap between being and
seeming. Duffy has a fondness for the movies too. But she uses
her film clips to zoom in on specific states of mind, particular
people. John Burnside's is the poetry of the tacit, the implicit. Of
the poets selected here, his disciplined brushwork is the deftest,
his verbal surfaces the most delicate. John Burnside is the book's
most 'domestic' poet and Home, whether in 'home rule' or the
search for roots or emotional stability, is certainly prominent in
this anthology. Burnside's homing instinct is pronounced, fervent
and quietly expressed. This is characteristic:

> Silence is possible, and after dark
> it almost happens: silence, like a glove,
> the perfect fit you always hoped to find.
>
> 'Silence is possible'

The serenely ontological poetry of John Burnside not only
demonstrates that silence is possible; it observes it.

Duffy and Burnside allow the reader to share revealing
vantage points from which a real but lost Scotland can be
glimpsed. Almost polar in their formal and tonal distance from
each other, these poets represent at times this anthology's two
governing tendencies. On the one hand, a public poetry, a
poetry of the state and its affairs that is often engaged and
frequently enraged; on the other a more private, ruminative and
detached verse, a poetry of dream. It's an over-simplification but
I think an allowable one to see these extremes in the poetry
produced in Scotland in the 80s and early 90s, and to see poem
after poem combining 'state' and 'dream' in differing proportions.
Naturally, this being Scotland 'whaur extremes meet' and where
the theme of 'doubleness' haunts our literature, these polarities
regularly collide in the work of the *same* poets. Whitman's
grandiloquent *carte blanche* 'very well I contradict myself. I am
vast. I contain multitudes' has never seemed to me adequate to
encompass the thrawn rivenness of the Scottish psyche. Carol
Ann Duffy for instance is at once a *performing* and a *confiding*
poet, one for whom Scotland is an emotional rather than intellec-
tual entity.

Attempts to encompass, understand and explain Scotland are central to the practices and procedures of the group of poet-critics associated with the magazines *Verse* and *Gairfish*. Although these writers do not represent any kind of formal grouping, various factors link the work of Robert Crawford, W.N. Herbert, David Kinloch, Peter McCarey, Alan Riach, and Richard Price. All have published books of criticism. All except Riach and McCarey edit literary journals. Edwin Morgan has taught some and influenced all of them. Each writes a vividly-voiced and individual verse. Yet in its intellectual breadth, confident absorption and redeployment of poetic source material (MacDiarmid and Morgan especially), its capacity for cosmopolitan sophistication and a very Scottish directness, its rapport with both Europe and America, its deep interest in popular culture, Scottish history and the mass media, above all in its conscious (occasionally self-conscious) ambition to be newly Scottish and yet unbounded, the poetry of these six writers does have a good deal in common. Price has dubbed this group the 'Scottish Informationists', though it remains to be seen whether the label will stick.

Robert Crawford, the most prominent of them, has the clearest and most carrying voice and is beginning to establish a place for himself outwith the literary world where he has made considerable impact both as poet and critic. Douglas Dunn included him in his Faber anthology. He appears also in *The New Poetry*. Dunn's work was an influence on Crawford's long before they became colleagues at St Andrews University after the older poet's very public and conscious decision to return to Scotland. Possessed of an uncommonly cheerful poetic disposition Crawford is inclined to hail rather than mourn the past. 'Opera', which demonstrates an almost Elizabethan relish for emblematic embellishment, brings together two of Crawford's preoccupations: industry and childhood. Remembering watching his mother working at her sewing-machine, the poet tells us:

> To me as a young boy
> That was her typewriter. I'd watch
> Her hands and feet in unison, or read
> Between her calves the wrought-iron letters:

SINGER. Mass-produced polished wood and metal,
It was a powerful instrument.

In 'Inner Glasgow', a sixties childhood of '*Look and Learn*' and 'pit bings' is contrasted with the de-industrialised present:

Where docks are cultivated, hard nostalgia
Steam-rivets us to ghosts we love,

In this Glasgow,

. . . everybody looks the same and sings
Of oppression, smokes, drinks lager, shouts out 'fuck'.

Typically however the poem *refuses* nostalgia, ending in affirmation: the adult will return to Glasgow to marry and to write.

Even stronger evidence of a new patriotism (by which I mean a clear-headed, historically sophisticated, sensitively *inter*nationalist and conditional affection for one's native place) is provided by Crawford's increasingly anthologised signature poem, 'Scotland'. Here, with a startling precision worthy of MacCaig, Scotland is seen from the air as a 'semiconductor country, land crammed with intimate expanses'. Instead of the lochs and brochs of conventional poetic diction, we find Scotland extolled in the jargon of the 'silicon glen' on which so much of our industrial future now depends. The poem's conclusion is one many young Scots are inclined to jump to,

. . . among circuitboard crowsteps

To be miniaturised is not small-minded.
To love you need more details that the Book of Kells –
Your harbours, your photography, your democratic intellect
Still boundless, chip of a nation.

In his bold appropriation of the technical to express his Scottishness, Crawford exhibits a pedigree that owes something to late MacDiarmid and middle-period Morgan. Knowledge, its acquisition, categorisation and transmission – the poetry hums with it. Much of it is of course owed to Scots who inspire Crawford to celebration as well as cerebration: Alexander Graham Bell; the founders of the *Encyclopaedia Britannica*, of the *OED*; J G Frazer, Logie Baird, Grierson, Reith, 'knowledge engineers' all, and many of them discussed in Crawford's prose book *Devolving English Literature* (1992).

Our immature and risible national obsession with the Scottish angle, our stolid determination to prove that even celebrities who are manifestly not Scottish can somehow be fielded in the Scottish team is hilariously sent up in Crawford's 'Alba Einstein'. Here the physicist is posthumously 'outed' as a closet Glaswegian inspiring the usual tacky panoply of identity-undermining cultural merchandising including 'the A.E. Fun Park', and 'Albert Suppers' complete with 'The Toast to the General Theory'. Aye, right enough! This is a woundingly witty poem about just how complex a collective inferiority complex can be. Crawford is comfortably, even ardently Scottish. Aware as a Scot of living 'between and across languages', he wastes no time debating which to use. Like all the poets in *Dream State* he uses the language that's to hand and most appropriate for what he wants to do. Of the comic potential which has always existed in the onomatopoeic expressiveness of Scots, he takes full advantage. By occasionally offering one of his Scots poems and a bathetically undermining 'translation' of it on the facing page, in the way for example that Gaelic verse is often presented, he not only reminds us of the essential untranslatability of poetry (though he is an accomplished 'owersetter' from other tongues), but also questions wider relationships between the English and the Scots. This typographical split-screen, much used by Ashbery and Derrida, gives a double emphasis to Crawford's point about the complexity of modern communications.

There was nothing complex however about 'Ghetto-Blastir', Crawford's mid-80s declaration of intent. It set out to cause a stooshie and did. The Scottish literary establishment at whom it was aimed got the message (very) loud and clear.

> Ghetto-makers, tae the knackirs
> Wi aw yir schemes, yir smug dour dreams
> O yir ain feet. Yi're beat
> By yon new Scoatlan loupin tae yir street

Crawford announced with a typically guileful play on dog's 'lead'
and poet's 'leid',

> . . . we're grabbin

> Whit's left o the leid tae mak anither sang
> O semiconductors, . . .

And that change is precisely what he and his peers have engineered.

W N Herbert, who though slightly younger than Crawford was
his contemporary at Oxford, publishing with him *Sterts and
Stobies* (1985), the shared pamphlet in which 'Ghetto-Blastir' first
appeared, handles Scots with even greater audacity. He argues (a
bit disingenuously one suspects) that his Dundonian provides a
S=C=O=T=S corollary to the L=A=N=G=U=A=G=E poetry
emerging in the US. Too much of his output is organised around
the personality of an identifiable seeing 'I', a poetic progenitor,
for it to qualify as being language-led. The temptation of his gifts
as a lyric poet of remarkable feeling and finesse are (thankfully)
too alluring. But in their aural veracity and lexical brio, his
experiments with the urban Scots of Dundee correspond to Tom
Leonard's pioneering work in Glaswegian.

The sharp, cocky, yet tender 'Eh' (Dundonian for 'I') of
Herbert's verse in Scots owes something to MacDiarmid on whose
poetry he has published a critical study, *To Circumjack
MacDiarmid* (1992), and to whom he offers homage in several
poems. It also owes something to the Americans, Ginsberg and
O'Hara, and even something to McGonagall whom he invokes in
poem after poem. Master of a pungent post-modern pawkiness (a
quality he shares interestingly enough with his fellow Dundonian,
the singer-songwriter Michael Marra) Herbert finds in the city he
left as a schoolboy a much more than local significance. Dundee,
which regularly deputises on film as an Eastern European capital,
is both more, and less, than Scotland, and as such well up to the
sometimes cosmic demands Herbert makes of it. Dundee is, as he
has delightedly noticed, an anagram of '*duende*', and Herbert's
work can be construed as a kind of Tayside *canto jonde*. For him,
as for John Burnside, Dundee is a place of 'provings'.

The 'Dundee Doldrums' written in his very early 20s after the
example of Ginsberg, anatomise the city magnificently:

Whaur ur yi Dundee? Whaur's yir Golem buriit?
Whaur doon yir pendies lurks it?
Broon brick, eldscoorit, timedustchoakit,
blin windies – whaur's MacGonnagal's hert?
'2nd Doldrum, Elephant's Graveyard'

Perhaps because his gifts are so many, so evident, and in inverse proportion to the notice they have attracted so far, Herbert takes a satirical interest in hierarchies and 'placings'. Though accomplished, Herbert's poems in English haven't quite the tang of his work in Scots. This places him at a disadvantage with critics outside Scotland. Many poems poke marvellously malicious fun at Scot Lit's High Heidyins and for all its mordant self-deprecation, 'Mappamundi', Herbert's 'poetic map o thi warld', exposes a real wound. Under the new dispensation, 'Ireland's bin shufted tae London' and 'Th'anerly ithir bits in Britain ur Oaxfurd an Hull.' A 'bittern storm aff Ulm' he may claim to be but his abilities and confidence move him closer to the centre of the literary map all the time.

Though anarchist in temper and a far from confirmed or conventional nationalist, Herbert (with his co-editor Richard Price) has used the magazine *Gairfish* to advance the cause of a 'McAvantgarde', one of whose most intellectually adventurous members is David Kinloch. An exact contemporary of Robert Crawford's, both at Glasgow and Oxford universities, and an editor with him of the international journal *Verse*, Kinloch writes a crammed, jammed, elusive poetry full of recondite Scots words and people, a poetry nonetheless capable of heart-tugging lyricism. Producing prose poems along more or less Rimbaudian lines *and* arias for the new Scotland, Kinloch (a university teacher of French) is a poet who has only recently found his own confident voice. Much of the explicitly and contentedly gay poetry Kinloch is now writing centres on 'Dustie-Fute', a juggler, an acrobat, a gay Orpheus, descended perhaps from Edwin Morgan's equally precariously poised circus performer, Cinquevalli. Certainly it is a relief (not just for him) that unlike Morgan he can write, as a *young* man, a poem like 'Warmer Bruder' at once a meditation of the fate of gay men in the concentration camps, a poem about Aids and a love lyric of understated power. Much more than 'simply' a gay poet, Kinloch is a *European* writer who has come home to Glasgow, and is determinedly saying for Scotland. 'The Tear in Pat Kane's Voice' ('tear' as in rip) reflects and adds to the *popular* culture of his city and his country.

> The tear in Pat Kane's voice
> Offers you a man's name,
> Whiter and harder than Alba:
>
> Adorno at his plain table,
> Rubbing out the barbaric lyrics
> Of post-Auschwitz poets

Like David Kinloch, Peter McCarey is steeped in French, making his living as a translator in Geneva. He also speaks Russian and developed his doctoral dissertation into a book, *Hugh MacDiarmid and the Russians* (1988). Sharing Edwin Morgan's love of Russian poetry and his keenness to translate from it, McCarey maintains a close link to Morgan that found practical expression in a series of collaborations in which the poets would take it in turn to 'deconstruct' a well known poem, publishing their versions together. These 'rehabs' as McCarey christened them demonstrate his quasi-structural passion for adaptation and renovation; for what's underneath. Thus the May 1968 graffito 'Sous les pavés – la plage' finds a poem springing up around it, one in which 'money is buying itself up'. This is also what's happening in the Glasgow of the Garden Festival, symbol of Glasgow's continuing, civic regeneration where some very ambiguous rehabilitation is going on:

> It's good: I don't have far to go
> from my refurbished close
> to see the butcher's apron on a sign set
> boldly in the weeping sump . . .
>
>   'Garden City'

His whole (unpretentiously) semiotic search for meaning is 'a sign set boldly in the weeping sump'. McCarey keeps a sceptical eye on the same spoiled and despoiled state as Carol Ann Duffy, the Britain of 'Wimpey Super Singles' and mass-communicated hucksterism whose motto could be 'it's what the people who want you to want it want you to want.' Such poetry can be too cranially crammed for its own good; and a lot of it operates at dangerously low temperatures. But McCarey's voice is worth straining to hear.

His Scotland (viewed from Europe) is a lot less enchanting than Crawford's, Herbert's and Kinloch's. As the US Marine points out to the Holy Loch protester who wants America's missiles sited in the middle of nowhere, 'Lady/I'm from Brooklyn: believe me/this IS the middle of nowhere '... On McCarey's 'Mappamundi', Scotland is wee and peripheral, its identity determined negatively in relation to what it's not, its existential benchmarks provided more and more by America. In 'Not Being Bob De Niro', McCarey mounts a neo-Thomist inquiry into Scotland's contemporary condition, setting out his stall at the same time.

> I want to do things that will
> last because they have
> substance as well as quality.
> Didn't Duns Scotus say that?

He did. But it sums up McCarey's credo, his celluloid-like capacity to capture and fix. Or as a whole short poem has it, 'OED' (Dictionaries again!):

> Every word in the language is laid out here
> with its meaning on a tag tied round its big toe.
> And here's me trying mouth to mouth.

These days Alan Riach's resuscitations are attempted from New Zealand, where he is a university teacher specialising in Scottish literature. He and Peter McCarey have a great deal in common. Both wrote doctoral theses on MacDiarmid. Both admire and correspond with Edwin Morgan. There's an ultra-contemporary, purposively fragmented cast to their minds. Neither has much time for notions of authorship pure and simple. Though stopping short (through a provident sufficiency of Scottish common sense) of naïvely accepting the structuralist slogans of 'the world as text' and 'the death of the author', Riach has worked witty and admiring variations on poems by Olson, Ashbery and Blackburn among others. These echo McCarey's rehabs and Herbert's 'doldrums'. Riach and McCarey have collaborated on a booklet-length philosophical detective poem too integrally dense and narratively ravelled to permit inclusion here. They are the most comprehensively 'post-modern' poets in the anthology. Yet for all that, Riach has a plain-spoken, sonorous, lyric gift. Whereas MacDiarmid allowed information to overwhelm the lyric in his later poetry, all the 'Informationist' poets seek to sing as well as tell.

Selectively influenced by America, it is not only when he is deliberately reworking Black Mountain or New York School poems, that Alan Riach adopts an American accent. In the way that many of our pop and rock and jazz singers do he absorbs *while* remaining sincerely his own man. The Ashberian plangency of 'The Blues', 'You're out there somewhere, going to a concert in wide company . . . ' is judicious and fine. Again like McCarey, Riach surveys Scotland from afar, in his case, Waikato. But for all the reminiscing, the evocations of childhood and loss, Riach has a classic Scottish immigrant's practicality and application. Allen Curnow can be heard in some of Riach's recent work. 'The Blues' is just one of the poems set in his adopted country that suggest that Riach has it in him to become an important *New Zealand* poet. But as a companionable and funny 'found' poem (not included here but well worth seeking out) reveals, he can still count on 'A Christmas Card from Edwin Morgan!'

The youngest of this loose grouping of 'Informationist' poets is Richard Price who is an editor both of *Gairfish* and of *Verse*. A curator in the British Library in London, he has published a study of Neil Gunn's fiction. Born in Reading, raised in Renfrewshire, his Scottishness is elective, discriminating and passionately energetic. Price's Vennel Press has published a number of the poets in *Dream State*. His poems have a taut and tantalising obliquity about them, a lyric leanness that compounds their emotional force. Family, married love, cars, buses and trains again and again return him to the question of identity.

> I'd have called it a 'flitting' but it was a year before I was born –
> to my father it was 'moving house.'
> He was Ma's envoy in Scotland:
> he'd just chosen a field
> that would grow into a bungalow

and he'd pay for it
whenever the bathroom,
opening on the hall
with a frosted glass door,
trapped her, towelnaked
before the postman
and something to be signed for.

'Hinges'

'Flitting' is just as evocative a word and concept for Price as it is for John Burnside. Busily editing and agitating in London, Price has become one of our envoys in England. His poem 'With is' ends with a characteristic sense of removal:

Our table is empty,
a summer curling pond.
Come on out on the town
(I've the nightbus map you lent me
when I was only a Scot)

Although he is a Doctor of Medicine rather than Philosophy, Iain Bamforth writes a well-read, uncompromisingly intellectual verse that's inclined to wear its learning brightly. While he shares philosophical, moral and aesthetic concerns with the poets considered above, he has published infrequent critical essays and edits no magazine. What really sets him apart from his contemporaries is his diagnostic gloom about Scotland, a dyspepsia he suffers more glumly than McCarey. Gramsci's 'pessimism of the intellect' has seldom been more balefully expressed. Crawford's 'optimism of the will' is mostly absent from these dour, dismal (and linguistically resourceful) poems. Bamforth's Scotland, a 'land of dissent and magnificent defeats', with its 'subtle theology of failure', a 'threadbare, ruinous country', where the 'servile myths, skite home' is a sermon his imagination broods on between sorties to Paris or New York, Polynesia or New Mexico. As widely read as he is widely travelled, Bamforth has a bulging steamer-trunk imagination. 'Alibis' features the 'ultimate collector', a figure whom this poet occasionally resembles. His Scotland has 'grown owlish with hindsight', a form of epistemological eyestrain these younger poets avoid, despite their close reading of Scottish history. Much exercised by his conception of Calvinist Geography, Bamforth puts theology to approximately the same use as Crawford puts technology. Like McCarey, he is an explicitly though not consistently post-modern poet interested in 'the semiotics of couscous' and 'the semiologists of bliss' and adrift in a world where recently it has 'all hardened into permanent lateness'. The arch, posed, Bohemianism of the poems he delivers 'in character' evoke not only the resilient Les Murray but also Ashbery or Ash at their most exquisitely salonesque and aphoristic – an almost gaudily gifted writer.

Kathleen Jamie's achievement depends less on the accretion of images and ideas than on their paring down. The honed flinty poems in *Black Spiders* got her noticed before she was out of her teens. She is one of the youngest poets in Douglas Dunn's Faber anthology and is part of the Scottish contingent in *The New Poetry*. There's a feisty candour to her work, a take it or leave it self-possession, a formal purity, that makes Jamie's the least paraphrasable, the most stripped down, the *sheerest* poetry in this anthology. Her collaboration with Andrew Greig, *A Flame In Your Heart* (not sampled here), in which she wrote in the persona of a nurse in love with, and pregnant by, a young Battle of Britain pilot (Greig), demonstrated a knack for monologue narrative and impersonation. Her own voice, whether in love, 'Things Which Never Shall Be', or in jest, 'Arraheids', in English, 'A Shoe', or in Scots, 'Xiahe', is attractive and assured. 'The way we live', Kathleen Jamie's best known poem, is looser and more headlong than a lot of her work; a joyous, jazzy inventory, it has affinities with the poetry of Morgan, and of Crawford and his ilk. Jamie's increasing fondness for Scots and her willingness to write explicitly about Scotland align her recent poems fairly closely with some of the writers considered above. She is however blazingly original. The staccato rhythms, the clear, curt, discourse, the juggling with the workaday and the wondrous – these mark Jamie out. It is in her work, that the disparate poetics of John Burnside and Carol Ann Duffy are most satisfyingly balanced.

Thus a beachcombed shoe on the shore at Cramond occasions first a meditation, then a declaration:

those shoes – stupid
as a moon walkers'; ah
the comfort of gravity.

The 'wedge of rubber gateau' becomes (literally) a 'platform' for affirmation:

God, girls we'd laugh –
it's alright once you're in
it's alright
once you're out the other side

Getting across is consistently a concern with Jamie. 'Permanent Cabaret', maroons its high wire artiste protagonist halfway, leaving her high and dry while:

The audience wonder: is it part of the show
this embarrassing wobbling,
this vain desperation to clutch

Jamie, too, 'knowing nothing of fear', will take 'sparkling risks fifty feet high'.

Another poem 'The Republic of Fife' finds her perched on her Fife rooftop, from which she can see 'Europe, Africa, the Forth and Tay Bridges'. Do *we* 'dare let go lift our hands and wave to the waving citizens of all those other countries'? Jamie's cosmopolitan and inclusive poetry is informed and often inspired by her journeys. Her travel prose is no less fine than her poetry. These fearless comings and goings sharpen her perspective on Scotland. Her tough-minded, though never flamboyantly intellectual verse, is as hospitably open and international as any currently being produced in Britain.

'Living in Berlin' and 'Poems of Departure' indicate that Elizabeth Burns, too, sees Scotland in context. Separation and suspension are recurring themes. In New York, 'in the place between daylight and darkness/in the place between your being here and leaving' the poet is 'wrenched between the old world and the new'. In Berlin she can see, 'wall's space like a tooth gap/explore soft new places with the tongue'. 'Valda's Poem', like several in this anthology, evokes MacDiarmid though it keeps him off stage. Here, it is his wife Valda who addresses us while Chris and Norman MacCaig make a recording indoors. What might have been a (justified) act of Feminist revisionism turns out to have no axe to grind. It's a dreamy but meticulous reconstruction of a moment and a mood, something at which this poet excels.

Angela McSeveney is a more forthright poet. Her recent first book was entitled *Coming Out With It*. And she usually is. Hers is the most autobiographically revealing poetry in this collection. Many of her poems were written in and about a severe psychological crisis and amount to a very moving record of a bout of self-administered psychotherapy. Utterly devoid of self-pity, they succeed (as similarly motivated explorations often fail to do) as poems *and* therapy. Nor is McSeveney's exploration of her self only psychological. Her work is full of proddings, partings and inspections. After the removal of a non-malignant lump in her breast, the fifteen year-old poet ponders her nakedness.

> I felt ashamed
> that the first man to see me
> had only been doing his job.
>
> > 'The Lump'

This most tactile of poets is always picking at her wounds. 'For the Best' recalls an actual sexual encounter punning with the phrase 'You rubbed me up the wrong way' in describing a cackhanded initiation. Size and sex are constant pre-occupations in McSeveney's poetry. Her customary tone in discussing these themes is one of a wryly protective self-deprecation as in the splendid 'The Fat Nymphomaniac's Poem'. Her Confessional candour allied to a sleekit sense of humour make Angela McSeveney a most engaging confider. That her poems are sparklingly clear makes being her confidant all the more pleasurable. She is not, however, her only subject. 'Night Shift' is a beautifully brought-off study in parental non-communication and 'The Pictures' tells a horrific tale with deadpan panache.

The openness and amiability of Jackie Kay's prize-winning *The Adoption Papers* was warmly praised when the story of her adoption as a black child by a white Scottish couple was published in 1991. Kay's expert handling of the poem's three voices – the two mothers' and the child's, her selection of telling detail, her narrative flair – these announced her as the intending dramatist she has since successfully become. Black. Lesbian. And a Scot: her status as an outsider is triply underscored. And yet hers is perhaps the friendliest and most 'upbeat' poetry in the book. A poetry that succeeds (as Liz Lochhead's does or as Tony Harrison's can) in being both consummate and popular. In its locus (The Campsies) and in its joyousness 'Pounding Rain' conjures up Morgan again:

> I stroked your silk skin
> until we were back in the Campsies, running
> down the hills in the pounding rain,
> screaming and laughing; soaked right through.

Fresh, chatty, funny, yet capable of great depth and seriousness, Jackie Kay's is one of the most hugely likeable new poetic voices. Her recent work not only consolidates her achievement but extends her range into a variety of genres and media: stage and TV drama, poetry for children, lyrics and social commentaries.

Also black, also lesbian, also living in England, Maud Sulter, a photographer and performance artist as well as a poet, has a less instantly recognisable voice, one influenced by a number of black American poets but a voice capable nonetheless of incantatory rage and tender fragility. 'As a Blackwoman' shows Sulter as angry, 'unpoetic' ('As a Blackwoman every act is a personal act'). Other poems are conventionally tender. 'Drich Day', a simple, sad, poem of leave-taking finds the poet and her loved one on the links at St Andrews with:

> nothing between us and Denmark
> except that tomorrow you leave me.

Much of Sulter's anger at sexual and class injustice is shared by Alison Kermack who instead of finding or cultivating a voice of her own, has simply (and effectively) taken over Tom Leonard's. This sounds strange; and is. But *what* she has to say survives the ventriloquism and Kermack's is merely the most extreme example of Leonard's influence on many young poets.

> it wiz hardur tay buleev in
> upwurdmubility
> when thay pit barbed wire

oan toappy thi lectric fens
thit ran roon thi skeem'

'Ikariss'

Meg Bateman's soulfully reflective poetry is at almost every conceivable remove from Alison Kermack's. Bateman's work, which I am able to appreciate only through its author's translations from the Gaelic, seems only circumstantially and incidentally contemporary: timeless verse written in but not always of, modern Scotland. Hers is in a particular sense a 'dream state'. Bateman's academic interests are in the Gaelic religious poetry written by women in the fifteenth century. Her rhymed metrical verse is cast in traditional forms whose force and felicity have been strenuously praised. Yet Bateman is a learner of the language, coming to it and indeed to poetry while at university in Edinburgh. That city forms the backdrop for much of her verse, a lot of it elegiac. Lost love and the adventures of an intricate heart are memorialised with almost Petrarchan dolefulness. But Bateman's passionate plaintiveness, the all too evident pain and searing sincerity, move and convince. In recent years, happiness in Bateman's personal life has kept her muse away. 'A Letting Go Of Dreams' reads worryingly like a letting-go of poetry.

No one man do I mourn
but a life-time's longing,
every unmade choice
slipping from me
because of you, fair man.

That loss would be *ours* to mourn. For Bateman is one of the most haunted and haunting of contemporary poets.

It is older Gaelic poets who appear to engage most energetically with the here and now, in particular, Fearghas MacFhionnlaigh, Crisdean Whyte and Aonghas MacNeacail. There are reasons of temper and tradition for Gaeldom's reluctance to modernise its poetic practices. The urge to preserve not merely language but form is understandably strong. Anne Frater (the youngest poet in *Dream State*), a writer from the same Lewis village as both Iain Crichton Smith and Derick Thomson is only slightly more 'modern' in outlook than Meg Bateman. At a time when Gaelic is *much* more discussed than spoken, she is, however, acutely aware of her cultural responsibilities. One might wish in fact for a little *less* responsibility and a little more youthful zest. With the recent Government investment in Gaelic television (bringing soap opera and other contemporary genres into the language) and renewed interest in Celtic music, there is an audience beyond Gaeldom for a poetry as open and accessible as Bateman's and Frater's. What is lacking in Scotland, as opposed to Ireland, is much sense of young writers using an ancient language to grapple with the present. A vehement and vocal nationalist, Frater has many contemporary concerns; her '9th November 1989', a celebration of the Berlin Wall's destruction, shows that the there and then (and the here and now) can be grist for young writers.

> An old woman comes
> to the Brandenburg Gate,
> which is not yet open
> as wide as the rest,
> a young soldier goes to her
> and she stands firm
> looking at her path
> laid out at her feet
> like steps of permission,
> pulling her,
> drawing her,
> and she moves again,
> and she watches the youth
> daring him
> to turn her back.

Maybe there will be less turning back in Frater's work in due course.

This predisposition is not confined to Gaelic. Writing in a lovely, unaffected, gravid Scots, the Fife poet William Hershaw displays a similar predilection for the backward glance. Given the scale and suddenness of the industrial change visited upon the mining, fishing and other industries of Fife, a tendency towards the elegiac is hardly surprising. Hershaw does, however, use the past to inform the future. 'Comp' poignantly memorialises Hershaw's grandfathers, Comp and Wull with their 'quiet and kenspeckle dignity'. What's being mourned here with and through, the passing of the two old miners, is the passing of a way of life. Of his place in the continuum of culture, community and family, Hershaw is acutely aware. 'They twa ware the making o me', he says attributing the 'sma worth' of his poems to his upbringing by his working-class parents. Given its restricted audience, all writing in Gaelic or Scots is an act of commitment. Well-versed in, and an adept translator from, the French poetry of the late nineteenth century, this poet is anything but unsophisticated. His commitment to birthplace, birthright and language is highly conscious. 'Januar Winds o Revolution', chides Fife and Scotland for their cowardice and complacency at a time when Eastern Europe was in ferment:

> The cauld wind o reality yowls sairly past the Labour Club
> Singan that in Prague, Berlin and Bucharest
> Are the fowk wi a speerit and smeddum.

Dreaming of a Scottish state, though in a more conventional Scots than Crawford or Herbert, Hershaw is a young Scottish poet readily prepared to assume with MacDiarmid 'the burden of a people's doom', while developing a sense of honest self criticism.

This birthright for the Shetlandic writer Robert Alan Jamieson encompasses not only poetry in the fertile language of his native island but experimental verse, plays and novels in English. Finding inspiration in MacDiarmid's sojourn on Whalsay Jamieson has written both poetry and criticism devoted to that poet. Jamieson's love of ideas, his tendency towards abstraction, his fearless and unembarrassed (and maybe even un-Scottish) willingness to 'think big' mostly finds expression in English. Only Jamieson, of the young writers gathered here, bears any trace of Kenneth White's influence. In his native tongue and with native themes, Jamieson is more earthed and earthy, producing a gloriously rich and mysterious Scots whose Nordic shimmer requires recourse to the glossary, even for readers familiar with the language. Most of what he has to say about Shetland's (or Scotland's) oil, he has said adroitly in prose, but the verse sequence 'A Day at the Scottish Office' lays bare the national psyche and psychosis with a twitchy quirkiness reminiscent of the Davids, Byrne and Lynch. 'Resistin the National Psychosis (9 April 1992)' is this anthology's only poem occasioned by John Major's unexpected election victory, a reversal much hated in Scotland:

I'm a diamond –
I will never fuckin crack –
Rough uncut and smaa
I roll aroond yer jeweller's scale
but I am unassayable –

Despite being less overtly political, the Paisley poet Graham Fulton comes on just as strong. He's read Bukowski; he attended workshops with Tom Leonard. You can hear them both in Fulton. But he has developed an original poetic personality that's aggressively his own. This is 'in your face' poetry, verse as stand-up comedy; even on the page every Fulton poem is a *performance*, while on the stage Fulton puts his work over with a pugnacity and aplomb uncommon among poets.

His is also a cinematic poetry, although this is a '*cinéma pauvre*' shot on 'super-eight', all grainy slo-mo and jumpcuts. Or then again, it can be grandiose and Cormanesque. But if Fulton is often Poe-Faced he is never po-faced. In Fulton's febrile imagination the television seems always to be on, spilling out Danny Kaye, or Neil Armstrong or John Boy Walton or The Monkees to take their chances with bit parts in a Fulton poetic snuff movie. Not so much post as hyper or mega-modern, Fulton's poems vibrate with a strobing, trippy sourness. Having been to the same America as Edwin Morgan, Fulton has brought back a scarier poetics. He is less a dream than a nightmare state. 'Charles Manson Auditions for the Monkees' represents a characteristic cultural conjunction (this one based on an actual event). It is also, like a lot of Fulton, tackily and blackly humorous:

Charlie wants
    to be an Axe-hero,
Charlie has mastered
    tricky chord changes,
Charlie has memorised lines
    that
the Beatles haven't written
    yet.

Emerging campily from the Golly Gosh Gothic of 'The Unmasking Scene' to wonder 'what I required to be an artist in the Eighties' the poet receives this answer:

> A vicious streak is
> fine and dandy
> a fucked-up life can
> come in handy

Quite. The grin-and-bare-it locale for these seamy shenanigans is a Los Angelised Paisley denied even the bilious bonhomie local boys John Byrne and Gordon Williams took refuge in. His Scotland often resembles Williams':

> We knew our country was a small time dump
> where nothing ever happened and
> there was nothing to do.
> And nobody had a name like Jelly Roll Morton.

Fulton's response to the various poverties around him is to hallucinate a poetry in which *anything* can happen, a verse which always has something to do – even if it's only striking attitudes all day.

Yet the anguish of real lives in hard times is not cheapened by Fulton's lurid posturing. His chippy lack of sentimentality, his excoriating ability not merely to describe but to *embody* frustration, the detached hipness of his technique, all these serve to amplify the scream. The width of contemporary Scottish poetry can be measured in the respective responses to de-industrialisation of a William Hershaw and a Graham Fulton. Where they concur is in their unwillingness to provide happy endings. In 'Goodnight John Boy', King Kong's demise is a reminder that, 'the bi-planes get us all in the end' a certainty that Fulton compounds by tailing off the poem in mid sentence.

Raymond Friel is an Irish Catholic from Greenock who favours simplicity in his discourse. His is another sixties Scottish childhood cooried into and picked over for succour and significance. In his poems we watch as Greenock is transformed from a forest of iron into a 'dole town'. Teaching now in London, Friel can get a good unmuzzy look at Scotland and its past, the rituals, observances and nuances of which he reconstructs tenderly. The lower Clyde he comes home to, in order to celebrate 'Hogmanay', is a place transformed by the loss of livelihood and way of life. And the identity-shaping folklore that died with it. The old myths and dreams no longer serve. A state of grace has given way to stasis.

Nowadays,

> We don't go in
> So much for myths,
>
> Believing more
> Often than not,
> That life's exactly
> What it looks like.

Don Paterson's is a world in which what you see is definitely what you get. The same age as Friel, he has already had his first volume made PBS Choice. His brusque, knowing tones are unmistakably contemporary. John Martyn's on the soundtrack. It's cool. Paterson is so cool he'll even interrupt his poems to make ludic, little post-modern guest appearances in them. Sometimes the poems seem to just scowl inscrutably, too mean to mean. None of which stops this being poetry of the first order. Paterson invites (and should fear nothing from) comparison with his English counterparts, Glyn Maxwell and Simon Armitage. The existential dreichness of Dundee and the wider world for which it acts as fall guy is caught precisely in the title poem of his first book *Nil Nil*. Paterson has configured Dundee as 'Undeed', a more torpid anagram than Herbert's *duende*. Life here is a goalless draw muddily slithered towards (Camus, never let it be forgotten, was a goalkeeper . . .). Paterson's Dundee, like W. N. Herbert's, is sometimes in America, sometimes farther afield. His verse dreams implausible connections:

> One day we will make our perfect journey –
> the great train smashing through Dundee, Brooklyn
> and off into the endless tundra,
>
> 'The Trans-Siberian Express'

After a long residence in Brighton, Paterson, a rock musician as well as a poet, has recently returned to his native city as writer-in-residence at Dundee University. His 'Amnesia' has moments of Bamforthian excess, a *mise en scène* of Fultonesque Grand Guignol, but remains acridly quotidian, its tone reasonable, everything leading us to the matter of fact last line 'It was a nightmare Don. We had to gut the place.' There are chasms beneath the glacial flatness of Paterson's poetic surfaces. That obsolete memento mori of an epoch, the elliptical stylus provokes a beautiful poem about his father (one which took third prize in the National Poetry Competition in 1991). The disruptive intrusion of another related poem into the one he has started, so far from seeming clever-clever, is sincere and moving, the circumstances of the elegy's making affecting and being included in what's made. The poem like the stylus, 'fairly brings out a' the wee details'. Paterson, stung by the memory of the shop assistant's condescension at his father's attempts to buy the old-fashioned stylus, ends the poem with the atypical avowal:

> I'd swing for him, and every other cunt
> happy to let my father know his station,
> which probably includes yourself. To be blunt.

To be blunt is something of a speciality with one of the youngest writers in *Dream State*, Stuart A. Paterson (no relation). His is a big-boned, firm-gripping, forthright poetry that's not above nuzzling the reader's ear. Paterson has no book of his own yet. But the range and assurance of his work bode well enough to hustle him into this one. So too with another Gregory Award winner, Roddy Lumsden, whom Graham Fulton could easily have accompanied, on 'The Misanthrope's Afternoon Walk'.

> They're all out today.
> The victims. The chipped on the shoulder.
> The chipped on the cheek, the scarred.
> The mental cripples. Baby mothers,
> Repros, pit bulls, tiny dummy-suckers,
> Bad moustached shouldn't-have been fathers.

Stylistically, 'Detox' seems to suffer its cold turkey under the influence of John Berryman and Carol Ann Duffy. Lumsden's Scotland is not particularly Scottish. The poems are worldly and unfazed, their ambience more redolent of Don Paterson than Stuart Paterson.

For all its swagger the younger Paterson's verse is genial, sentimental and oddly innocent. His skilfully expressed affection for Kilmarnock and its environs calls to mind Stewart Conn. He

stravaigs with the wide eye of a Burns or a Whitman. His poetry
loves and learns:

> At seventeen I kissed a date ON THE TIT!
> Twenty-one she was, immensely-nippled, almost
> (But not quite) able to feed me, suckling, snorting away.
> Mouths were irrelevant as we freed them to grab at
> The mysterious sculpting and folds of flesh.
> I tried to kiss her goodnight one time, she laughed
> And groped me. Kissing was never the same.

A love poet of unabashed candour, Paterson can also manage
satire. 'The Leaving of Scotland' set on Ne'erday 1997 has
Scotland asking for and being denied political asylum. Here is a
dream state that sleepwalks. Explicitly nationalistic, it's appeal-
ing, though less crafty and crafted verse, than the comic cuts of
Robert Crawford or W.N. Herbert. As I said before, *blunt*. But
a poetry brave enough to dream of,

> a country so awake that dreaming is for the sleepless.

* * *

Scottishness, in poetry, as in everything else, is a hard quality to
pin down. The novelist and screenwriter Alan Sharp has described
coming from Scotland as being 'a very specific existential event'.
Each poem in *Dream State* is that certainly. But in a country as
small and complex as this one, being more specific is difficult. As
Alastair Reid has pointed out, any statement about Scotland is
likely to be true; and just as unlikely to be the whole truth.

The whole truth is not to be found in this anthology. But the
poets in it are true to their times and their talent. This means
ignoring the tyranny of either or: not Burns, Dunbar; Muir versus
MacDiarmid; Scots or English; free verse as opposed to rhyme –
phoney dilemmas every one. Instead, following Morgan's exam-
ple, these poets want it all. But if their poems are inclusive, they
are also choosy. Their pluralism does not break down into a
semiotic void in which everything signifies, nothing means, and

anything goes. Every poet in *Dream State* writes to *communicate.*
   In a world obsessed with information gathering and Communications, poetry's best hope is to provide more compelling information, to communicate more engagingly. These poets do that. They are also to an unprecedented degree, with the exceptions noted above, interested in the here and now which MacDiarmid's 'Gairmscoile' seemed to forsake.

> For we ha'e faith in Scotland's hidden poo'ers,
> The presents theirs, but a' the past and future's oors

Goethe's advice to the young poets of America, offered a century before MacDiarmid's *Penny Wheep*, seems more apposite. He bade them,

> concentrate on the present joyfully

Dream State reclaims the present. There is a renaissance going on in Scotland across all the arts. The word culture is on the unlikeliest of lips. But we shouldn't have a culture instead of an economy or a parliament. A fully authentic culture requires a fully authentic politics; and a fully authentic politics requires a state.
   The Dream State offered here, is vibrant and various, self-confident and self-critical. It knows its past and claims its future. Above all it is vigorously alive in Scotland's noisy and numinous now. It's like the modern Scotland Edwin Morgan was talking about: a Scotland no longer riddled with questions of identity, whose citizens just happen to be, and are happy to be, Scots. As 'King Billy', one of the Morgan poems many of these writers studied at school, has it.

> Deplore what is to be deplored
> and then find out the rest

The rest, or some of it, is *Dream State.*

Carol Ann Duffy

Carol Ann Duffy

'I was born in Glasgow in 1955 and lived firstly in the Gorbals and then in Nitshill, a place name which, I remember, embarrassed me then! My family moved to England in the early 1960s and I spent most of my childhood in Stafford, feeling very much an outsider and trying to change my accent to sound like the English kids. In 1974 I went to Liverpool University, to read Philosophy, and from 1978 have been a full-time writer. I've written a few plays for stage and for radio, but this work has always been secondary to my work as a poet. I moved to London in 1982 and have lived there since then. The poems chosen for inclusion here reflect my concerns for identity ('Originally'), and the way we use the language ('Mouth, With Soap') and with the effects of time on our lives ('The Captain of the 1964 *Top of the Form* Team'). I suppose the short lyric, 'Plainsong', brings all these concerns together. I'm not a poet who feels comfortable writing *about* their own work. I hope that, when it works, it speaks for itself. '

Publications:

Standing Female Nude (Anvil, 1985)
Selling Manhattan (Anvil, 1987)
The Other Country (Anvil, 1990)
Mean Time (Anvil, 1993)

As editor:
(for teenagers)
I Wouldn't Thank You for a Valentine (Kestrel, 1992)
Speaking a Word of Dead (Kestrel, 1994)

Poet For Our Times

I write the headlines for a Daily Paper.
It's just a knack one's born with all-right-Squire.
You do not have to be an educator,
just bang the words down like they're screaming *Fire!*
CECIL-KEAYS ROW SHOCK TELLS EYETIE WAITER.
ENGLAND FAN CALLS WHINGEING FROG A LIAR.

Cheers. Thing is, you've got to grab attention
with just one phrase as punters rush on by.
I've made mistakes too numerous to mention,
so now we print the buggers inches high.
TOP MP PANTIE ROMP INCREASES TENSION.
RENT BOY: ROCK STAR PAID ME WELL TO LIE.

I like to think that I'm a sort of poet
for our times. My shout. Know what I mean?
I've got a special talent and I show it
in punchy haikus featuring the Queen.
DIPLOMAT IN BED WITH SERBO-CROAT.
EASTENDERS' BONKING SHOCK IS WELL-OBSCENE.

Of course, these days, there's not the sense of panic
you got a few years back. What with the box
et cet. I wish I'd been around when the Titanic
sank. To headline that, mate, would've been the tops.
SEE PAGE 3 TODAY GENTS THEY'RE GIGANTIC.
KINNOCK-BASHER MAGGIE PULLS OUT STOPS.

And, yes, I have a dream – make that a scotch, ta –
that kids will know my headlines off by heart.
IMMIGRANTS FLOOD IN CLAIMS HEATHROW WATCHER.
GREEN PARTY WOMAN IS A NIGHTCLUB TART.
The poems of the decade . . . *Stuff 'em! Gotcha!*
The instant tits and bottom line of art.

Translating the English, 1989

'. . . and much of the poetry, alas, is lost in translation . . .'

Welcome to my country! We have here Edwina Currie
and The Sun newspaper. Much excitement.
Also the weather has been most improving
even in February. Daffodils. (Wordsworth. Up North.) If you like
Shakespeare or even Opera we have too the Black Market.
For two hundred quids we are talking Les Miserables,
nods being as good as winks. Don't eat the eggs.
Wheel-clamp. Dogs. Vagrants. A tour of our wonderful
capital city is not to be missed. The Fergie,
The Princess Di and the football hooligan, truly you will
like it here, Squire. Also we can be talking crack, smack
and Carling Black Label if we are so inclined. Don't
drink the H$_2$O. All very proud we now have
a green Prime Minister. What colour yours? Binbags.
You will be knowing of Charles Dickens and Terry Wogan
and Scotland. All this can be arranged for cash no questions.
Ireland not on. Fish and chips and the Official Secrets Act
second to none. Here we go. We are liking
a smashing good time like estate agents and Neighbours,
also Brookside for we are allowed four Channels.
How many you have? Last night of Proms. Andrew
Lloyd-Webber. Jeffrey Archer. Plenty culture you will be agreeing.
Also history and buildings. The Houses of Lords. Docklands.
Many thrills and high interest rates for own good. Muggers.
Much lead in petrol. Filth. Rule Britannia and child abuse.
Electronic tagging, Boss, ten pints and plenty rape. Queen Mum.
Channel Tunnel. You get here fast no problem to my country
my country my country welcome welcome welcome.

Originally

We came from our own country in a red room
which fell through the fields, our mother singing
our father's name to the turn of the wheels.

My brothers cried, one of them bawling *Home*,
Home, as the miles rushed back to the city,
the street, the house, the vacant rooms
where we didn't live any more. I stared
at the eyes of a blind toy, holding its paw.

All childhood is an emigration. Some are slow,
leaving you standing, resigned, up an avenue
where no one you know stays. Others are sudden.
Your accent wrong. Corners, which seem familiar,
leading to unimagined, pebble-dashed estates, big boys
eating worms and shouting words you don't understand.
My parents' anxiety stirred like a loose tooth
in my head. *I want our own country*, I said.

But then you forget, or don't recall, or change,
and, seeing your brother swallow a slug, feel only
a skelf of shame. I remember my tongue
shedding its skin like a snake, my voice
in the classroom sounding just like the rest. Do I only think
I lost a river, culture, speech, sense of first space
and the right place? Now. *Where do you come from?*
strangers ask. *Originally?* And I hesitate.

Ash Wednesday 1984

In St Austin's and Sacré Coeur the accents of ignorance
sing out. The Catholic's spanking wains are marked
by a bigot's thumbprint dipped in burnt black palm.
Dead language rises up and does them harm.

I remember this. The giving up of gobstoppers
for Lent, the weekly invention of venial sin
in a dusty box. Once, in pale blue dresses,
we kissed petals for the Bishop's feet.

Stafford's guilty sinners slobbered at their beads, beneath
the purple-shrouded plaster saints. We were Scottish,

moved down there for work, and every Sunday
I was leathered up the road to Church.

Get to Communion and none of your cheek.
We'll put the fear of God in your bones.
Swallow the Eucharist, humble and meek.
St Stephen was martyred with stones.

It makes me sick. My soul is not a vest
spattered with wee black marks. Miracles and shamrocks
and transubstantiation are all my ass.
For Christ's sake, do not send your kids to Mass.

The Way My Mother Speaks

I say her phrases to myself
in my head
or under the shallows of my breath,
restful shapes moving.
The day and ever. The day and ever.

The train this slow evening
goes down England
browsing for the right sky,
too blue swapped for a cool grey.
For miles I have been saying
What like is it
the way I say things when I think.
Nothing is silent. Nothing is not silent.
What like is it.

Only tonight
I am happy and sad
like a child
who stood at the end of summer
and dipped a net
in a green, erotic pond. *The day*
and ever. The day and ever.

I am homesick, free, in love
with the way my mother speaks.

The Captain of the 1964 *Top of the Form* Team

Do Wah Diddy Diddy, Baby Love, Oh Pretty Woman
were in the Top Ten that month, October, and the Beatles
were everywhere else. I can give you the B-side
of the Supremes one. Hang on. *Come See About Me?*
I lived in a kind of fizzing hope. Gargling
with Vimto. The clever smell of my satchel. Convent girls.
I pulled my hair forward with a steel comb that I blew
like Mick, my lips numb as a two-hour snog.

No snags. The Nile rises in April. Blue and White.
The humming-bird's song is made by its wings, which beat
so fast that they blur in flight. I knew the capitals,
the Kings and Queens, the dates. In class, the white sleeve
of my shirt saluted again and again. *Sir! . . . Correct.*
Later, I whooped at the side of my bike, a cowboy,
mounted it running in one jump. I sped down Dyke Hill,
no hands, famous, learning, *dominus domine dominum.*

Dave Dee Dozy . . . Try me. Come on. My mother kept my mascot
  Gonk
on the TV set for a year. And the photograph. I look
so brainy you'd think I'd just had a bath. The blazer.
The badge. The tie. The first chord of *A Hard Day's Night*
loud in my head. I ran to the Spinney in my prize shoes,
up Churchill Way, up Nelson Drive, over pink pavements
that girls chalked on, in a blue evening; and I stamped
the pawprints of badgers and skunks in the mud. My country.

I want it back. The captain. The one with all the answers. Bzz.
My name was in red on Lucille Green's jotter. I smiled
as wide as a child who went missing on the way home
from school. The keeny. I say to my stale wife
Six hits by Dusty Springfield. I say to my Boss *A pint!*

How can we know the dancer from the dance? Nobody.
My thick kids wince. *Name the Prime Minister of Rhodesia.*
My country. *How many florins in a pound?*

Mouth, With Soap

She didn't shit, she *soiled* or *had a soil*
and didn't piss, *passed water.* Saturday night,
when the neighbours were fucking, she *submitted*
to intercourse and, though she didn't sweat cobs then,
later she *perspired.* Jesus wept. Bloody Nora. *Language!*

She was a deadly assassin as far as
words went. Slit-eyed, thin-lipped, she
bleached and boiled the world. No Fs or Cs,
Ps and Qs minded, oh aye. She did not bleed,
had *Women's Trouble* locked in the small room, mutely.

In the beginning was The Word and, close behind,
The Censor, clacking a wooden tongue. Watch out
for the tight vocabulary of living death. *Wash out*
your mouth with soap. She hoovered on Sundays, always,
a constant drizzle in her heart; below it *The Big C,* growing.

The B Movie

At a preview of That Hagen Story *in 1947, when actor*
Ronald Reagan became the first person on screen to say
'I love you, will you marry me?' to the nineteen-year-old
Shirley Temple, there was such a cry of 'Oh, no!' from
the invited audience that the scene was cut out when the
film was released.

Lap dissolve. You make a man speak crap dialogue,
one day he'll make you eat your words. OK?

Let's go for a take. Where's the rest of me? *'Oh, no!'*

Things are different now. He's got star billing,
star wars, applause. Takes her in his arms.
I'm talking about a *real* weepie. Freeze frame. *'Oh, no!'*

On his say-so, the train wipes out the heroine
and there ain't no final reel. How do you like that?
My fellow Americans, we got five minutes. *'Oh, no!'*

Classic. He holds the onion to water such sorrow.
We need a Kleenex the size of Russia here, no kidding.
Have that kid's tail any time he wants to. *Yup.*

Politico

Corner of Thistle Street, two slack shillings jangled
in his pocket. Wee Frank. Politico. A word in the right ear
got things moving. *A free beer for they dockers
and the guns will come through in the morning. No bother.*

Bread rolls and Heavy came up the rope to the window
where he and McShane were making a stand. *Someone
sent up a megaphone, for Christ's sake.* Occupation.
Aye. And the soldiers below just biding their time.

Blacklisted. Bar L. *That scunner. Churchill.* The Clyde
where men cheered theirselves out of work as champagne
butted a new ship. Spikes at the back of the toilet seat.
Alls I'm doing is fighting for wur dignity. Away.

*Smoke-filled rooms? Wait till I tell you . . . Listen,
I'm ten years dead and turning in my urn. Socialism?
These days?* There's the tree that never grew. *Och,
a shower of shites.* There's the bird that never flew.

A Shilling for the Sea

You get a shilling if you see it first.
You take your lover to a bar nearby, late evening,
spend it all night and still have change. If,

if it were me, if it were you, we'd drink up
and leave; screw on the beach, with my bare arse
soaked by the night-tide's waves, your face moving
between mine and that gambler's throw of stars.

Then we'd dress and go back to the bar, order
the same again, and who's this whispering filthy suggestions
into my ear? *My tongue in the sea slow salt wet . . .*

Yes. All for a shilling, if you play that game.

Plainsong

Stop. Along this path, in phrases of light,
trees sing their leaves. No Midas touch
has turned the wood to gold, late in the year
when you pass by, suddenly sad, straining
to remember something you're sure you knew.

Listening. The words you have for things die
in your heart, but grasses are plainsong,
patiently chanting the circles you cannot repeat
or understand. This is your homeland,
Lost One, Stranger who speaks with tears.

It is almost impossible to be here and yet
you kneel, no one's child, absolved by late sun
through the branches of a wood, distantly
the evening bell reminding you, *Home, Home,
Home*, and the stone in your palm telling the time.

John Burnside

John Burnside

' I was born in Dunfermline, in 1955 and lived in Scotland for most of the next ten years. When I was eleven, my family moved to an industrial new town in England; I was very much affected by the move, and have not forgotten the feeling I had of being uprooted from my community, and from the dialect and local landscape of Fife.

I am primarily a poet, though I have written some short stories, mainly for radio. I am very interested in the prose poem as a form – I find it surprising that so little prose poetry is written in English. In *Common Knowledge*, and *Feast Days*, I explored the prose poem in a number of pieces, and I imagine I will continue to return to this form as it can be a very rewarding discipline.

As far as my work is concerned, I feel there are real dangers in trying to summarise a position or an approach to poetry. I do not consider myself to be a nature poet, for example, though I make frequent reference to the natural world; I would not describe myself as a psychological or philosophical poet, though I am occasionally interested in the nature of the self; I would decline to be classified as a religious poet, though my work will sometimes explore spiritual matters, especially the notion of the soul, and the powerful images of rebirth and renewal in the resurrection story. But all these concerns are intertwined. All I can say of my work is that I am responding to the world into which I am constantly arriving, and which I find consistently mysterious; I am concerned with myth and language, faith and loss; with trees, water, earth and frost; with the seasons, and images of rebirth and renewal. For me poetry is a discipline and a quest which does not end, but continues, beyond the personal, beyond what I imagine I intend. '

Publications:

The hoop, (Carcanet, 1988).
Common Knowledge, (Secker and Warburg, 1991).
Feast Days, (Secker and Warburg, 1992).

forthcoming:

The myth of the twin, (Cape, 1994).

Two saints

My first school was a wooden bungalow
named for Brigid, patron saint of wells.
I thought she must be cold, like the closed spring
that whispered in the wood behind our house,
but later I was told of sacred fires
deep in Kildare, where monasteries were built
according to Pope Gregory's decree.
The elder Brigid glimmered in that land:
a motion under flames, the shifting greens
of dark and bright, bound in a speaking hearth.
I felt time shatter when the Normans came.

Lessons went unlearned. I played a part,
scratched the twelve times table on my cuffs
and copied spelling lists from hidden books.
But I was thinking of the undergrowth.
There would be dreams and Brigid would be there;
blue as rain her firelight on my skin.

One day I helped my father clear a pond.
We drew rakes through the water, gathered weed
and raised it dripping, shot with sudden light.
The weft was heavy, tugging for its depth.
Spread on the path, it shone like new-dyed silk.

That year we moved. There was another school:
red brick walls, locks and window bars.
It echoed like a vault when we ran out
to Christmases; the waxy corridors
swarmed with Roman numerals and names.
Saint Columba's High. If there were tales
of wicker furnaces and holy wells
I have forgotten them.
Every month we had a class exam:
History was statute books and wars,
Sixteen Hundred to the present day,
never reaching now. I started French.
All I knew of that school's saint was this:

that it was he who gave the people
books and silence at the story's end
and on an island sheltered from the stream
he drowned the oracles in chiselled stone.

Dundee

The streets are waiting for a snow
that never falls:
too close to the water,
too muffled in the afterwarmth of jute,
the houses on Roseangle
opt for miraculous frosts
and the feeling of space that comes
in the gleam of day
when you step outside for the milk
or the morning post
and it seems as if a closeness in the mind
had opened and flowered:
the corners sudden and tender, the light immense,
the one who stands here proven after all.

Cow Parsley

That was another country
where anything might be
concealed frog-chill or adder,
blisters of golden spawn.

A spiderling domain where shade
thickened and settled,
and we ran barefoot into dreams
of lime and cuckoo-spit.

We took it to contain
a foreignness: the undergrowth of forms
we chose to fear,

black fingertips and wings; rust-printed nails
and crouching versions of our secret selves
beneath the froth, all knowing looks and smiles.

'Silence is possible'

Silence is possible, and after dark
it almost happens: silence, like a glove,
the perfect fit you always hoped to find.
But somewhere close a child is whimpering;
like the sound of a backstreet violin
the wind is everywhere, repetitive
and incomplete. Sirens are wailing
all over the city. New snow creaks
under leather. Silence is possible,
but you have been a listener for years
and what could you find but the hard quiet
of huddled swimmers in a riverbed
or the casual hush of abattoirs
after the thud of a bullet nobody heard.

Urban Myths

The secret versions of ourselves,
truthful because they seem
remembered: laughing children
hidden amongst lupins,
cars by the roadside vanishing in fog:

and terrors we meant to avoid
tracking us through a long
acquaintance:

blood on the kitchen floor, blood in the roof;
networks of bone and nerve in drifted leaves

snagging the rake; a perfume of resurrection
filling our throats, sweeter than we expected,
the scent of a garden surrendered to someone else,
the ghosts in its shrubbery only this moment's loss:
a life recalled, that could not happen now,
like summering elms, or the Jesus who walks in carols.

The Noli Me Tangere Incident

There was nothing to touch. The smell of daybreak tinted
with frankincense; the feel of an empty sheet and something
slipped away; a moment's unidentified blackness receding
among shadows. She waited. After some time there were
cries and threats, memorised wounds, the taking of deposi-
tions. They spoke of flesh, they gathered with the dead, but
she remained in the cool garden, trying to place the voice
that had gone before her to the still centre of the shade,
fixing in her mind the sound like poured water and the black
footprints rising through gravel; a hint, perhaps, or only a
supposition; nothing you would mistake for resurrection.

Anamnesis

Memory, you should have known,
is a double agent:

One of those gaberdine
people in films, a smiling

Harry Lime. It leads you
through scalars and cosines

to the murmur of cuckoo clocks.
It leads you

into a sewer. You strike
matches and the rats

squeal. Up ahead
someone is splashing away

through grey water. A hurried
figure you know from somewhere,

splashing and stumbling
into the flashlights and guns.

Exile's Return

Hard to imagine it, lying intact,
folded into books: identity
to be assumed like tartan,
or spelt out on museum clocks
from heretic stones and peat-blacked pots,
history by strip light. Do we know
where we are in these tourist hills?
Is it plantain we chew to draw the taste
our childhood was? The soft, even names
come easily, we have the voice for them, we know
the stories of threadwork and burning turf
and supple hands that gather in a storm.
And when we reach the narrow, choppy loch
we remember the legends of giant fish
that no one believed and everybody told
as we drove south that morning, years ago,
pretending we could find our own way home.

Source Code

The same life happens again:
a city of clocks and leaves
delivered through fog,
bakeries, print rooms, the famille verte
of municipal gardens
continued, the way a memory runs on
from somewhere unrecollected
and vast,
how you always imagine the suburbs
busy with bonfires and hymns
at Halloween,
when every house is lit, a déjà-vu,
leading through street names and churchyards
from nothing to nothing.

Out of Exile

When we are driving through the border towns
we talk of houses, empty after years
of tea and conversation;
of afternoons marooned against a clock
and silences elected out of fear,
of lives endured for what we disbelieved.

We recognise the shop fronts and the names,
the rushing trees and streets into the dark;
we recognise a pattern in the sky:
blackness flapping like a broken tent,
shadow foxes running in the stars.
But what we recognise is what we bring.

Driving, early, through the border towns,
the dark stone houses clanging at our wheels,

and we invent things as they might have been:
a light switched on, some night, against the cold,
and children at the door, with bags and coats,
telling stories, laughing, coming home.

Domestic

Late afternoon in October:
light feathers the kitchen walls,
finds long-lost cousins
in saucepans and colanders.
Footballers slide back and forth
on the muddy distance,
their voices splashing the neat
straight-furrow rattle of tractors
like slops. The new ram
is penned in the yard:
biblical in his hard
angle of heat and smell
and over-cautious, he stands
bowed, as if space itself
kept changing and had to be learned
in shifts and slants.
We sit indoors, alone,
pressed to the silence
like wasps to a window pane.
 If we think of the homes we have known,
or stops between tunnels
when silence steps up to a train
through frost-printed trees,
if we think of old lovers or schools,
blank fields of ragwort and stones
or moss-scaled crab-apple lanes,
it barely shows.
At teatime, lamps go on
across the valley.

The marmalade cat stares in
from the window's gloaming
and, watched, we become what we seem
in the moth-coloured light,
like these figures we make in glass,
irredeemably bright.

Peter McCarey

‘ "Not Being Bob DeNiro" is ugly and frustrated, and it doesn't sort itself out till near the end. Like the other poems of mine that Donny O'Rourke has selected, it was written as I realized I was surplus to economic requirements in Scotland. All right, with a bit of wit I might have found work there, but I've always preferred to save my wit for the page. 'Beware of Trojans Bearing Title Deeds' deals with two types of foreigner: the conqueror and the immigrant. ('Terroni' is a north Italian word for southern peasants, a bit like 'teuchter' for a Highlander.) The title is adapted from a wise Trojan's opinion of the wooden horse the Greeks had left: 'Beware of Greeks bearing gifts'. Aeneas the Trojan escaped and went a-conquering in Italy.

It seems that when the students of Paris howked up cobblestones to make barricades in May '68 they found a layer of sand underneath; they took this as a sign: dismantle civilization and life becomes idyllic – 'sous les pavés–la plage'. Had they dug through the sand they'd have found the usual sewage system.

Like me, my poems have moved away from Scotland. An 1100-liner I wrote last year shows the Three Wise Men (an arms dealer, a robot and an unsavoury piece of genetic engineering) blundering round Europe and Africa. I like retorting to other writing – revamping older texts or replying to other writers. I see literature as a slow conversation, and now that I'm living in a country that doesn't know what Scottish English is, it's become very slow indeed. I'm often talking back to people who are dead, so I don't hold my breath waiting for a response. What do I write for? To touch your heart, as a good poem will; it should be like hearing a familiar cadence in a far place, or – as I did recently – coming across the grave of a Scottish infant (Elizabeth Livingstone) in Botswana:

> Lisa, Lizzie, Betsy, Beth,
> a stony dream, an early death;
> your mummy's gone and this is the hand that rocks you.

> Elizabeth, in this place
> the full futility of talking
> has dried my lips until they crack in song. ’

Publications:

Hugh MacDiarmid and the Russians (Scottish Academic Press, 1987)
For What It is, co-written with Alan Riach (Untold Books, 1988)
Town Shanties (Broch Books, 1990)
Bad Roads (forthcoming, 1994)

Not being Bob DeNiro

A colour supp. feature on Robert DeNiro –
about, more like: they could pin nothing on him.
"All our negociations were done on the phone"
Who pays the actor
calls the shots. It's nothing personal.
Highly professional. Bang.
And then, as Jakobson says,
To attribute the feelings expressed in a work
to the author
makes as much sense as mystery play mobs
beating up the actor who played the devil.
If you're convinced, then so am I.
The mediaeval mob is on this bus, though,
reading about someone who won't be drawn
on who calls up the demon in the cage of light.
It's us that let you command those fees;
we trade our cash for folding plush
to see you, and we want to know
just who you think you are, and what
the hell you think you're playing at.
"I want to do things that will
last because they have
substance as well as quality".
Didn't Duns Scotus say that?
And how d'you get substance onto film?
The only substance is celluloid, – light,
if you count it as particles. Look at him there,
beating against that bright screen.
They can't even give him a definite shape.
People get so used with TV dinners
they think the packaging's what's underneath.
It gets gummed up, scar tissue to bone;
frozen or burnt to the throwaway ashet.
What's underneath this 9to5 job
that I'm trailing round like a ball and chain?
For don't you forget that as long as I loathe it,
it is not me and I am not it.
Go on, settle down to the company motor,

step on the gas of the global economy.
Money can buy you happiness (it says
in this ad for a fancy Toyota).
See if I pay just the V.A.T.,
can I get the happiness and leave the hardware?
No? then I'll have to drag it about
and the weight of the world if need be because
I am not it and it doesn't own me.
You don't believe me. You're looking askance
or over my shoulder (get back to your crossword) –
He's got a job and a wife and a kid
and a house and a car and a notion to write.
I play golf myself; gets me some fresh air.
Great he's on xxK bloody yuppie
dinky moaning about no having time to write
because he's a wageslave.
Why doesn't he go on the bru then and write
about what it's like to be unemployed?
If I was on the dole I'd be writing, so
I wouldn't be unemployed.
I've got to come to some arrangement
and this way I still have one way out:
getting off the bus, though if I do that
then I'll soon be a stat in a government scheme.
O so he's admitting he could be worse off
after all he could be out sleeping rough
or nailing up curtains, keeping a family
on moonlight and supplementary.
That's right: this way I've got leisure to moan
so from your way of seeing it,
no right to do so. Away back to Possil.
The video van's on its way.

In the supp there's this photo of Robert DeNiro
what's that in his jacket – a passport?
"He's Italian, he's American, he's perfect"
I was Scottish, but British, imperfect
tense, writing not to be written out.
"Then the door flies open and he bursts in from nowhere"
So what but. What do you mean so what?
A lot of folk bought this paper;

most of them probably read this, it's
the piece with the biggest picture and fewest words.
"He was thin; his face was gaunt.
When he came back two and a half months later
he was a different man. He looks 20 years older
He's put on 30 pounds."
Three pound a week: that's a strain on the heart.
Phantom parturition of selves
that life had left on the cuttingroom floor.
Turn time into space and lives
'll look like olive trees: pruned back
and cracked with the weight,
rerouted, culdesacked in shapes
they're not quite conscious of;
the level of sap in the lung of this tree
is conscience, me, the present tense.
The bus I'm on pulls in to the stop
and the traffic lights go to green.
Curdling smoke carved up in the headlights.
I say to myself: if we're stuck at this junction
I'll be stuck in this job for good.
The last one gets on, the lights go to red,
the bus pulls out and goes through them. So:
there'll be some hitch, some unorthodox move
to make, some rules to break, but I'll get clear.
I hadn't, actually, counted the queue,
I didn't know the sequence of the traffic lights either:
a moment's gamble it was. And yet
I did have an idea of my surroundings
and in some way this moment
shapes the next, the intellect and will.
Look into the branching light
where, stripped of substance, good and evil
can play at sticks and stones and break no bones.
"He knows it's a performance,
so he can be as villainous as the part calls for."

Beware of Trojans bearing Title Deeds

The rain the wind turbines
the clouds the rain comes
clattering down through dams
Namibian metals rot at Dounreay
the coal at Seafield. We worked there a
mile out under the sea and on Sundays
or whenever the day off was, I don't remember
what he said (remember it, remember! that
's what this is FOR) we took the bus or we
walked and we sat there on the sea cliffs in
Fife and we looked at the sea we looked at the sea.
When a man died down there his mates
would keep him down until the end of the shift
so the widow would get his full day's pay.
So the management
brought in a doctor
to ascertain the time of death
and that was when he was paid till.
From the Highlands and Ireland
from Poland and Lithuania. They worked outwith
their majesty's tidal sway neither on nor under
the land. This isn't blood and soil,
nor yet a notion
grounded in shared speech, says one whose forebears
came up the Clyde on a bike.
Terroni who took ship (the Anchor Line,
I guess) for New York, and disembarked at Finnieston
with some equally wandered Jews. Paddy's Milestone,
Ellis Island; the Statue of Liberty? well,
it's like on a peace march to Dunoon a friend of mine accosts this
Marine and says to him look,
if you have to have your rotten missiles
why can't you keep them somewhere safe,
in the middle of nowhere? and he says 'Lady,
I'm from Brooklyn; believe me,
this IS the middle of nowhere' . . .

Garden City

I met an alkie, I dispensed the small change,
he set aside the small talk and said, "Listen,
I'm a very good person, you know",
which is to say: Possessions and professional
skills are not of the essence;
I am.
So I said "Yes" and went away,
which is to say: The unsure strain of such awareness
is left to the likes of you. I want my tea.

It's good: I don't have far to go
from my refurbished close
to see the butcher's apron on a sign set
boldly in the weeping sump, the tobies and broken brick
where head-high rosebay willow herb
with clover, jaggy nettle and soothing dock
festoon and cloy the legend
WIMPEY SUPER SINGLES AND
1, 2 AND 3 BEDROOM FLATS
SELLING TO COMMENCE SHORTLY
or, in a city brasserie,
the porous tit on a plaster cast
poke out from ivy tumbling off a period cuspidor.
It's what the people want. It's what
the people who want it want. It's what the people
who want you to want it want you to want.

Sous les pavés – la plage

The urban sunlight comes in the window
staggering up to its knees in sand
banknotes blowing out of its seams
like scarious leaves and carious buildings
shaking dust from my shoes but it cloys,
it clogs for I'm paid to be here.

Frontiers, harbours, roads, currencies,
crowd control and corpse disposal.

Money is busy buying itself up
using what there is for collateral.

Light is said to be sculpting itself
with its only sense
of touch.

O.E.D.

Every word in the language is laid out here
with its meaning on a tag tied round its big toe.
And here's me trying mouth to mouth.

Alan Riach

❛ I started writing verse at school but the earlier impact was visual, not literal. Words came with school, dictionary exercises done during playtime: I loved learning new words, and like anyone else of that age, learned words for notions then new to me.

There was also an early disjunction of language. When I was four, my father became a pilot on the London River and we left Scotland. I went to school in Gravesend, in Kent, but my parents and I and later my sister returned to Scotland for every holiday. I write in English, but the English I write has never belonged to England. Scotland was always home and still is. I still speak with its voice.

I returned to live in Scotland after I'd completed my schooling and first degree at the University of Cambridge. I studied for the doctoral degree at the University of Glasgow, in the Department of Scottish Literature. Glasgow was and still is the city I most enjoy being in. The city's West End, as John Purser has said, is the best-educated constituency in Britain and conversations flourish in divers locations. Friendships too.

When a post-doctoral research fellowship came up at the University of Waikato, Hamilton, New Zealand, I saw the advertisement in a newspaper. I remember typing the application on my grandfather's old portable Remington. I now work there as a lecturer in the English department. What happens next I don't know. ❜

Publications:

This Folding Map (Auckland University Press, 1990)
An Open Return (Untold Books, 1991)
Hugh MacDiarmid's Epic Poetry (EUP, 1991)

Editor of the fourteen-volume edition of Hugh MacDiarmid's *Collected Works* (Carcanet)

At Loudoun Hill

At Loudoun Hill
in its sleep
on the Strathaven Road
on the dreamy edge of Ayrshire
and Lanarkshire,
                    in one of the many
corners of this folding map,
where incidental blood once streaked the grass,
and I can't remember now what time
of day it was or even
if I read what time of year –

  It would be cold, like this,
sunlight like teeth, and the yellow grease
on swords and harnesses; even now –
that horse over there: its teeth
have the colour of the day,
and its sound –

                    By Loudoun Hill, now,
between Arran and Strathaven,
between the submarines and the frigates
and the gardeners and the forget-me-nots
and the profiteers and the ignorant;
between Arran and the leafy burghs of small-town
Scotland, half-awake, if only that,
where (my Grandfather told me) the only
excitement seen in the streets
was the fairly regular visit of
the hearse . . .

                    By Loudoun Hill, its odd isolate
            shoulder-shape
            in the Farmers' fields
            in Lanarkshire, in
            the Common Market.

I was driving back,
from Arran, and
the sight of it passing
my shoulder made me think a
little about the trip, and I
couldn't imagine I had
made it alone. What does it mean
to be so modern
                    at Loudoun Hill?
with the smell of cow
dung and horsebacks,
the sheep's wool toughness in the grass,
the blotched cows in their loneliness,
the colours in the landscape mainly easy, mostly
tonally the same: redundant greys,
redundant greens. Only
the shoulder
of the hill goes into the wind, goes
                    into the mind
like another thing,
        like you pass through a door
and it's another place, there is something 'still strong
still unflinching in spirit'.

So I stopped the car
and I stood there with a gaunt eye, but not, now,
watching the armies of men on the hillside
and the men on the level fields
preparing their senses and their long blades getting
keener,
but looking at a recent incremental recognition
of who was never there, but holds it
all in balance, now, at Loudoun Hill,
                    money-eyed,
    watching.

The Heron

To you who are long gone
and far away
       I send
these words, rolling down and round the world.

For answer,
you'll send midnight to me from your distant place
and I'll return it.
And nothing more will ebb away.

Like the heron Diarmid heard
that had landed on a rock off Ireland
(when Grania at last overtook him
they heard it cry at break of day
in the tidal air while the sea swept past
in the bitter cold, and she asked him why
it gave that cry?
– It is frozen to the rock, he said.

– I stand rock-hard in this stony place
and the soft diurnal sift
that will ash rock
strains me to you, and I lean
but do not loosen.

A short introduction to my Uncle Glen

Glen was always building sheds. He'd buy
wood. He had a thing about building sheds. He built
six stables in his garden, then realized
he'd have to buy the horses for them (and did). He built at least
three aviaries and more kennels than I can remember.
He filled the aviaries with parrots and canaries
from Australia, Pacific Islands. He always
had dogs: Alsatians, a Great Dane he would dance with

around the kitchen, before he was married. Now,
his kitchen cupboards are full of his kids' litters of Jack Russells.
He used to like Lonnie Donegan.
He used to play the guitar and yodel like Frank Ifield.
At every piece of news today you tell him
he looks amazed and shakes his head and says: 'My, my!'
A couple of years ago some of the family took a week's
holiday in Tenerife. Glen was walking on the beach
with my father, talking. Apart from the army,
when he'd been in England and learned to be a chef
(and cook these great sweet yellow curries)
he had never been out of Scotland much. He said
to my father, 'Jimmie,' (which is his name) 'you've sailed about
the world a few times.' (Which is true.)
'Tell me,' he said,
'Where exactly are we?'
Surely,
it's the best way to travel.

North

The fishes' sightless eyes, drowning,
Cast back upon cold waves
(– The cranners would not have them –)
Whirl the stony world around them,
Like a revolving stone axe,
Swinging like a great fowl caught up in a storm,
All flesh and seed
And pebbles like round, hard eggs,
Making a circle like Scotland's sound.

Hard and swift and sharp,
The red knife's silver blade
Halves mackerel on a plate glittering with scales.
The knuckles gutting wedge and grate.

The sculling fleeing claws,
Wound on the flesh of the angled god,
The Osprey, taut strength beating

Wings over bare spears of stalks
Waving on a crofter's site.

– Scotland is surrounded on all sides with sea,
Except one, to which it bears
A proximity much like a candle
Burning brightly in the black eye-socket
Of a tremendous skull.

They dream only of Scotland

(after John Ashbery)

The dreams they dream are only of
Scotland to be looking for it through
hundreds of islands and millions
of acres of gorse, to be tasting
this honey is delicious, but it
burns the throat
                    Or hiding from twilight in offices
(they can be adults now, all grown up)
and the murderer's swagger is easily
seen in the shadow on the oblong, lilac loch.
He holds keys in his right hand.
                              – That was before
we could drive for miles, for hundreds of miles
at night on roads through bracken, and when my headache grew
worse, would stop
at a petrol station. Now I care
much more about signs. What sign
does the honey give? What
about the keys?
                    I am going into the bedroom slowly
                    I would not have been hurt
                    had I not fallen against the
                    living-room table. I am back
                    against the bed, doing nothing
                    but waiting in the horror of it
for our liberation, and lost
without you.

The Blues

The lights are on all over Hamilton.
The sky is dark, blue
as a stained glass window in an unfrequented church
say, by Chagall, with grand and glorious chinks
of pinks and purples,
glittering jewels on those glass fronted buildings
where the lifts are all descending
and the doors are
being closed.
           You're out there somewhere,
going to a concert in wide company or maybe
sitting somewhere weaving a carpet
like a giant tapestry, coloured grey,
pale brown, weaving the wool
back in at the edges of the frame, your
fingers deft as they turn the wool in tight and
gentle curves.
           Or somewhere else.
           What do I do
           except imagine you?
           The river I keep crossing
           keeps going north. The trains
           in the night cross it too.
           Their silver carriages are blue.

Elizabeth Burns

Elizaberth Burns

' I was born in 1957, grew up in Edinburgh, did an English degree in St Andrews, and have worked in a variety of jobs. I've also been involved in various ways – through publishing, editing, writing workshops etc. – with women's writing, and am interested in the question of an identity for women working in what has been the mainly male domain of Scottish poetry.

My poetry reflects this interest in women's ways of seeing and writing. 'Valda's Poem/Sleevenotes', for instance, takes the context of the Scottish poetic tradition and wonders how it might appear to a woman looking in from the outside; while 'The Poem of the Alcoholic's Wife' is based on the life of a Finnish poet. I'm interested in how this links in with the idea of an unwritten history, of trying to recover, or rediscover, things which have been lost or forgotten, perhaps because they've been seen as female and insignificant.

I'm also interested in writing about the unseen, the ways in which people communicate with one another in ways which are often intuitive, outside the realm of language and so can move through boundaries of time and space, or across political barriers like the Berlin Wall (that poem was an 'imagined' one, written two years before the wall came down).

My poetry aims in some ways, then, to put into words things that might not have been said before, giving voice to people who may have been silent, and making what was invisible, visible through words and images. '

Publications:

Poems (pamphlet) (School of Poets, 1986)
Ophelia and other poems (Polygon, 1991)

The Poem of the Alcoholic's Wife

Not just the endless empty bottles
the beery taste of kisses;
not just the stench of the bedroom
where his vomit smears the floor;
a cupboard stuffed with secrets
smashed china
photographs ripped from their frames

But, somehow, as well as this
a memory of myself once
in a yellow cotton dress
a breeze off the sea
and his hands gently touching my face;
and of my mother in a corner of the kitchen
writing her journal

and now, a woman who brings me oranges;
a poem thought up in the night
forgotten over breakfast
as the nuzzling child tells of her nightmare
then dragged back by a bunch of lilacs
plucked in the rain
and quickly recorded on a typewriter
balanced on the lap

Living In Berlin

used to be a street here / this is where I used to live
old man slumps / lost in wasteground grass

war's gone / but city still has bare patches
bombs under rubble / miserable widowers

cold war begins / no one dies by fire any more
this is the place where / wall will be built

wall splits the city / wall is graffitied
wall is laughing / but enormous

this is where you will live / these are the people who
but what if – / the one I love is –

wall is erected / she plans tunnels
dreams of wings / imagines people on the other side

paces her segment of the city / until
she reaches wall / flaunting itself

time comes when wall / goes out of fashion
is broken down / brick by brick

and then such a seeping and merging of split city
it seems there are fields opening up and it's greener

and more spacious on the new un-walked down
        labyrinth of streets
with their untouched buildings and their different
        smells

in a café she's discovered on the other side
he turns and offers her his pale green wine which she

sips and in his garden there are white poppies
ripe raspberries they eat with buttermilk

in afternoons full of sweet fruit tastes
and in warm evenings they stroll out over city

see wall's space like a tooth gap
explore soft new places with the tongue

Poems of Departure

I
in the dream we are in New York   walking the
    humid streets
under an orange sunset   blurred with smog
but the houses seem too old and foreign   to belong
    here
we cannot find   5th avenue   east 12th street
and everywhere's too quiet and too beautiful for
    New York City

an old man with a horse and cart   shuffles past
along deserted gutters   selling white roses

it becomes in the dream   a city of the old world
of quaint houses   the scent of roses in the streets

Europe and America   split by an ocean   the two of us
wrenched between   the old world   and the new

II
I feel as a child about to be abandoned
who screams at her mother 'I don't love you anyway'
I have a stack of sharpened words inside me
that I pull out to wound you with
make little nicks in your skin
instead of kisses   but at the same time
I want to be curled in the crook of your arm
I want things like lullabies and cocoa
an abundance of tendernesses

III
of these last days together I will remember
the motherly holding of one another
the placing in my lap   of the grey and white shell
that you found on the beach at Ardalanish

and your calm voice reading poetry into the night
keeping sadness at bay   though how sibling close it
  creeps

until its breath is all over me   inside my imagination
making the tears come at my throat   a blue-grey
  sobbing

IV
fat globe   I want to punch you
batter away   at your enormity
I hate you for the   gaps you make
for your infinite   wildernesses
of continents   and oceans
you smug   plump   planet

V
I dream of infidelity   of a woman who discovers
her husband's unfaithfulness abroad
knots silk scarves together   into a noose
pulls it tight   around her neck

VI
we are living in a limbo   in a half life
in the almost colourless place   where the limp tongue
of the last of day   licks the sky with faint colours
slight flickers   of green or apricot
these are the shades   we live with
in the place between daylight   and darkness
in the place between your being here   and leaving

VII
the white candle of our last evening   still burns
the white flowered violet that you gave me   blossoms
light falls   on your gift of the rose garden painting

the room is ghosted   with your presence
and remembrances   pungent as rosemary
seep through   the muslin of the heart

Sisters

Even when she moved
five hundred miles away
telepathy was alive between them
and love as strong as ever

She sends in the post
pressed tulip petals
slivers of shell from the day at the beach
wrapped in tissue paper

She, a book of stories
golden earrings

and she, the painting of a windy day
the daffodil bowl

Even before the letter
saying, between the lines, 'come',
she is on her way

Valda's Poem/Sleevenotes

Sleevenotes to Hugh MacDiarmid's record Whaur Extremes
Meet:
*'Recorded at Brownsbank, the home of Valda and Chris
Grieve, near Biggar in the Lanarkshire hills on two sultry
days in June 1978. Chris, in his chair by the window, talking
with his friend, the poet Norman MacCaig, a wee dram in
every glass. Valda in swimsuit, working in the garden, or
keeping the soft-coated Wheaten and Border Terrier quiet
for the recording.'*

June sun presses on my back as I bend
sweat gathers at my neck and under my arms
I am naked as I can be in my bathing costume

I step out onto the flowerbeds
making light footprints with my bare feet
Spray trails from the watering-can
falls in dark circles round the plants

I want to lie out on the parched grass
and let the sun's hands touch me everywhere
let them finger the frail flesh of my breasts
rub gold into the crease and wrinkle of my stomach

At the open window edged with ivy
they sit, two old men in their shirt-sleeves
On the table between them a bottle of whisky
the two fat volumes of collected poems
and a tape-recorder lapping up their words

The dog flops in the shade of the back door
I go to her when she stirs, stroke her hot fur
give her water, keep her from barking

I hear their talk and laughter, his and Norman's
I hear the rise and fall of Chris's voice
the rhythms of his favourite poems, over and over

In the afternoon I sit against the apple tree
feeling the dent of bark on my bare shoulders
I close my eyes and the murmur of their voices
blurs with the birdsong that maybe
when we listen to the finished record
will have swum inside the poems

William Hershaw

William Hershaw

' I've lived mainly in Fife. Cowdenbeath, Inverkeithing, Lochgelly, Burntisland, Dysart: these place names make better poetry than any I can write. My mother and father both came from big mining families – my mother was one of eight, my father had three sisters and eight brothers. Both my grandfathers spent their working lives down coal pits and my father's brother John was killed in one. I was never near a pit till I went on holiday to Wales and visited a tin mine.

I started writing poetry when I was seventeen because I was an inarticulate bag of nerves but I still liked to get the last word in. Neil Young and Bob Dylan were a bigger influence than Burns and Chris Grieve. My first attempts were in a strangulated form of English but I relaxed a bit when I found a form of Scots closer to my heart and thoughts, closer to though not the same as my own speech. Poems are organised language designed to create an effect and even Tom Leonard's are artificial.

I like to think I write to sustain the decent and humane values of the people I was brought up among. I try to be a joiner with words because I regret not having a trade. There are dangers in this. You can romanticize your past or write about it in an unquestioning way. You can be labelled 'New Kailyard'. You need to be an intellectual to let such criticisms bother you though – how to spell Scots or whether it is valid to write in it are issues that pass me by.

Like a lot of not very clever people I ended up at university. I didn't like it there. Now I'm an English teacher – not Mother Teresa but still useful. Teaching and writing poems both pass things on and I think the past is important. I try to give the bairns value for money and I've got better at it since I had two of my own. '

Publications:

High Valleyfield (Urr Publications)
Glencraig (Urr Publications)
May Day In Fife (Scrievins Press)
Proverbs o Hell (Scrievins Press)

Comp

Aince I haed twa grandfaithers,
Noo I hae gotten nane.
Auld Wull I scrieved o no lang syne
Noo by and by I cam tae mourn anither ane.

Auld Wull and Comp were like the day and nicht,
Ane wes dour, ane douce.
Tho' baith haed warked thir life ablo the grun',
Auld Wull haed taen the coal-bleck tae his natur'
While Comp blinked bonny in the sun.

Baith were straucht and true
In the wey maist miners hae,
Thon quiet and kenspeckle dignity
(But Comp forby wes gentle tae).

He taught me dominoes and cairds
And mair asides. Noo ay allooin
Fir fause sentiment that follys deith,
The plants he settled wi his haunds
Are ayeways grouwin.

I ken fine that in some timeless airt
Lang eftir closin 'oors has cam,
We'll lift anither haund o banes,
Me wi ma pint, him wi his rum.

Fir there is a licht that nivir gans oot,
There is a licht that nivir gans.

Tae Ma Mither and Faither

Honest, hard-warkin, warkin-class Fife fouk,
Son and dochter o miners theirsels,
Brocht me up tae hae

Faur mair than they,
Forby, tae mind whaur I cam fae as weill.

Langtime it's taen me tae cleirly see,
So reader be mindit that if ye speir
Owre whit sma worth
These wards hae got –
They twa were the makars o me.

Johnny Thomson[1]

Johnny Thomson, lithe as Spring
An athlete and a goalkeeper
Wha could save onythin'
But wan wanchancy kick tae the heid
And the lave o a young life
Gi'en scant time tae floor.

Yet ye can still fund auld men
Wha walked tae his funeral in Cardenden[2]
Wha's faces wull bloom owre and een
Moisten at memries o days lichtened;
Brocht fae Brigton,[3] means test[4] and dole
Bi his gracefu dives and shut-oots.

Johnny Thomson, in the thirties
Minded naethin' fir politics or bigotry
And lay deein at Ibrox park;
Ahent him at the Rangers' en'
The hoots and jeers grouwin like weeds
Wad hae drooned oot the crood at Nuremberg.

---

[1] Celtic goalkeeper accidentally killed in a match against Rangers in the Thirties while diving at the feet of Rangers player Sam English.
[2] Mining village in Fife, birth place of Thomson.
[3] Brigton Cross near Parkhead in Glasgow.
[4] Whereby the unemployed underwent a thorough investigation to find out whether they would receive state assistance.

On Hearing the Psalms Sung in Gaelic

I hae heard them sing
Like a hert-sair bairn desertit bi its faimly.

I hae heard them sing
Sad as the wund, bleak as their corrugated kirk.

Their singin was like ma sowel torn fae ma chist
Tae spake afore me in God's leid.

They sang wi a holy dreid
That tell't o a' they'd lost.

The kythin wards unkent tae me but the hale
Hauf-kent, a tale mindit fae bairnhood.

I hae heard them sing,
Noo I maun believe their tungue was spake
In whit Eden[1] there ever was.

Januar Winds o Revolution

From A Calendar o a Seaside Toun

A cauld, sleety wind angles doon the High Street.
It blaws aff the Forth and ower the Links,
Past the butcher's, the bookies, the pub and the Store.
It rattles the lichts on the toun Christmas tree,
It birls the newsagent's sign aroond,
It blaws like a wild Blake picter
On this mirkfu januar efternin.
The Siberian wind kyths fae an airt lang held in ice
And has blawn whaur a biggin-wa's ca'd doon.
It has blawn whaur a playwricht's heezed up president,

---

[1] Many Gaels believed their language the original one, spoken by Adam and Eve.

It has blawn ower a tyrant's bluidy heid,
Through a year o revolutions.
It blaws fae the Kremlin ower the Lammerlaws
And through the tuim heids o Burntisland fowk
On its road ti Glesgi. Syne we craw
At the deith o Socialism and nivir speir oor thirldom.
We blaw o oor culture capital – hot air.
The cauld wind o reality yowls sairly past the Labour Club
Singan that in Prague, Berlin and Bucharest
Are the fowk wi a speerit and smeddum.

Robert Alan Jamieson

❛ Born in Shetland in 1958, I grew up in Sandness on the west mainland with no other children my age around me for the first seven years, in a large extended family. My grandfather was once the county librarian, while my mother was a dedicated writer of letters and journals. So writing seemed a natural thing to do, and my childhood stories and poems allowed me to people the solitude. After a wandering down a few adolescent cul-de-sacs, like dropping out of university, my mother's early death spurred me to give up an oil-company salary to write full-time, publishing two novels, *Soor Hearts* (Paul Harris, 1983) and *Thin Wealth* (Polygon, 1986), and a collection of poetry, *Shoormal* (Polygon, 1986). At the end of this first intensive burst of work, I felt 'written out'.

So in 1988 I went back on the learning curve, studying language and literature at Edinburgh University, which was a great experience. I realise now I had carried around an anti-academic resentment for a dozen or so years. Overcoming that liberated me and my writing. My third novel, *A Day at the Office* (Polygon) which weaves poetry through its narrative, was published in 1991. Other work includes the libretto for a symphonic cantata by David Ward, two plays, and translations from Danish, Czech and Ukrainian.

Coming from a community which has a limited literature of its own but having already gone beyond its parameters, I don't feel I have any direct literary forebears, though in recent years I've realised I'm part of a Scottish tradition, like it or not. MacDiarmid's time in Shetland is a strong connection; though our linguistic roots are different, I identify with Iain Crichton Smith's ambivalence over exile from the island and native language; I recognise much in George Mackay Brown's landscape, but Shetland and Orkney are really as different as Edinburgh and Glasgow. The worlds of Scandinavian writers like Knut Hamsun or William Heinesen are as familiar.

There are many fine writers I respect, both dead and alive, male and female. If I have to name names, then I'd say my first crush was on R.L.S., while my first real passion was Hamsun. Lately I've grown to love W.S. Graham. But saying that little hardly defines what I do, and denies a thousand affairs with words from all over the world . . . yes, even England . . . . ❜

Sang oda Post War Exiles

Harry listen Harry please
We canna bide nae langer.
Da aert is tired man, sae is du,
We'll sell da sheep, we'll sell da coo.
Gie up da lease.

Come man awa
For we maun ging
Across da Soond o Papa

Harry listen Harry please
Du'll git a better job.
Somethin maer reglar, wi reglar pey,
Dis croftin wark, hit'll never pey.
Life wid be aesier.

Come man awa
For we maun ging
Tae a cooncilhoose in Scallwa.

Meg Meg, du canna ken,
Du døsna understaand.
Foo muckle dis is pairt o me,
Dis affbidden bit o pøramus laand.
Hit gies me strent.
Hit gies me stimna.

T'Scallwa Castle

Quhitever shite drappt oot dy privvies
Still maer bed on ahint, inside de,
In da trots an haas an guts
O da Stewart clan at aaned de.

I canna celebrate dy stonn in ony tongue
Nor care tae rub da green fae yon bress plaet
Da National Trust sae carefilly hae nailed ta de.
Fir evry chisel swap, a bairn gret oot fir maet.
Fir every stonn lade t'dy foond, anidder stonnless
Grave wis fillt wi benklt brukkit bens o fok
Still young if de an aa dy hertless kyn hed
Only hed a tocht bit eence fir somethin idder
Dan dir gut-fat laanded swallys an dir privvy shite.

19.11 hrs.

Sit doon wi hot news dinner,
a microwoven a la carte delicht
laek the ad-folk aet.
ah coont calories in captions,
watch the screen version o ma food
while chowin owre the events
o a day at the Scottish office.
Whit's new? A plane has crashed,
a politician lied,
an actor wrote a book.
The day is different fae the ithers
by dint o the head-talkin's tie,
the time telt by the season's cut an colour
by ma empty plate.

22.59

an ah hae seen life the nicht,
happenin elsewhar,
hae listened tae a hunder folk
spaekin owre the issues
currently in vogue,

aa happenin elsewhar.
Roonded up an rationalised,
it maks a tidy pile o plastic
in the tv company file:
a record of our time
the voice of our time
a sign of our time
the cause of our time
view and counterview
a tale of lust and greed
of passion's thrusting hand
and what it grasps
Language gougin memory, music gaugin mood
the documentary evidence o whit its laek tae live the day
elsewhar

Resistin the National Psychosis
(April 9th 1992)

I'm a diamond–
I will never fuckin crack–
Rough uncut an smaa
I roll aroond yer jeweller's scale
but I am unassayable–
Rockin in the gyral cradle
I'm unassailable–
a speck o haillness, fixed an stable–
my name is single caa
I'll answer tae–
I bear nae makar's braand–

I love the puzzle madness poses
tae yer need fir diagnosis

Robert Crawford

' I was lucky. Though neither of my parents was particularly interested in writing, they had a respect for books, and encouraged my rabid fondness for reading. Though I'd made up stories since pre-school days, by my mid-teens it was poetry that obsessed me. At school I had some excellent English teachers. I'd malinger with them after classes, talking about T.S. Eliot in order to avoid going to maths. The alluring music of Eliot's poetry convinced me, even when I couldn't follow what was happening. A wee poser, I sat reading *Four Quartets* on the blue train home from school in Glasgow. I wrote nothing but sonnets then, and thought this ought to attract girls.

When I was eighteen, I went to Glasgow University to study English. I showed some poems to Edwin Morgan, who encouraged me and later gave me MacDiarmid's poems (largely new to me). I got involved for a short spell with a small magazine in the university, and enjoyed reading widely beyond the course, and listening to visiting writers, but I avoided any writing groups. By that stage I'd started to publish in magazines (especially Duncan Glen's splendidly supportive *Akros*), but my poems were still immature. I wanted to publish a book.

A scholarship took me to Oxford to write a doctorate (eventually I dumped Tennyson for T. S. Eliot). Being in that alien environment – the first time I'd been outside Scotland for more than a few days – made me think hard about what and how much it meant to me to be Scottish. I wanted to write a poetry that relied on Scottish resources, without undue chauvinism and with a sense of humour. Out of that came the poems of *A Scottish Assembly*, though many of these were written after I'd come back to Scotland in 1987. I knew I had to repatriate myself, go for what I really loved.

In 1988 I married a girl I'd known as a student at Glasgow. Since 1989 we've lived in St Andrews where I teach Scottish Literature at the University and co-edit the international magazine *Verse*. Sometimes there are odd cross-fertilizations between my academic work and my poetry. The poetry tends to go ahead, like a sniffer dog, and the academic research gets pulled after like an anxious handler. For instance, my prose book *Devolving English Literature* was bound up with an evolving vision of a multilingual, pluralist Scotland that came out of *Sharawaggi* and

Talkies. The writers I consider in *Identifying Poets* and in other books and essays are ones I admire.

I write about people and things I love. Phrases and images start a poem off, often earcatching or eyecatching juxtapositions – a satellite dish on an old croft. Poetry like people comes in all shapes and sizes. It belongs to the imagination, and so to everybody. Imagination is what powers people and society. I'd like to write a four-wheel drive poetry (like that of Les Murray) that could go into all sorts of territories, and go there with a big audience. A four-wheel drive double-decker bus is what I'm after. **)**

Publications:

Poetry: with W.N. Herbert, *Sterts & Stobies* (Obog Books, 1985); with W.N. Herbert and David Kinloch, *Severe Burns* (Obog Books, 1986); contributor to *New Chatto Poets 2* (Chatto, 1988); *Other Tongues: Young Scottish Poets in English, Scots and Gaelic* (editor, Verse, 1990); *A Scottish Assembly* (Chatto, 1990); with W N Herbert, *Sharawaggi* (Polygon, 1990); *Talkies* (Chatto, 1992).

Prose: *The Savage and the City in the Work of T. S. Eliot* (OUP, 1987); *About Edwin Morgan* (co-edited with Hamish Whyte; EUP, 1990); *The Arts of Alasdair Gray* (co-edited with Thom Nairn; EUP, 1991); *Devolving English Literature* (OUP, 1992); *Reading Douglas Dunn* (co-edited with David Kinloch; EUP, 1992); *Identifying Poets: Self and Territory in Twentieth-Century Poetry* (EUP, 1993); *Liz Lochhead's Voices* (co-edited with Anne Varty; EUP, 1993).

Opera

Throw all your stagey chandeliers in wheelbarrows and
    move them north
To celebrate my mother's sewing-machine
And her beneath an eighty-watt bulb, pedalling
lambs on an antique metal footplate
Powering the needle through its regular lines,
Doing her work. To me as a young boy
That was her typewriter. I'd watch
Her hands and feet in unison, or read
Between her calves the wrought-iron letters:
SINGER. Mass-produced polished wood and metal,
It was a powerful instrument. I stared
Hard at its brilliant needle's eye that purred
And shone at night; and then each morning after
I went to work at school, wearing her songs.

Inner Glasgow

You were a small red coat among the pit bings
That aren't there now, between Cambuslang
And Shettleston, with *Tell Me Why, Look and Learn*;

The quays have altered, liners replaced by jasmine;
Where docks are cultivated, hard nostalgia
Steam-rivets us to ghosts we love, in murals

Where everybody looks the same and sings
Of oppression, smokes, drinks lager, shouts out 'fuck'.
Shops sell us. Entrepreneurs' industrial

Museums postcard grime; we're pseudo-Griersonned.
But you refuse these foisted images, stay
Too true, still here, grown up in your red coat.

My inner Glasgow, you don't leave me, I
Do not leave you. A tubular steel frontage, roadcones
Flash towards us like the tiny folded pictures

In pop-up books, the lovely, lovely details
Too close to label art, that bring on laughter
When words cut out their starter motor, leaving us

Idling beside a cloudless firth. Those shorelights
Spread beyond Millport, beckon us to marry,
To lie along the bowsprits of our lives.

Scotland

Semiconductor country, land crammed with intimate
    expanses,
Your cities are superlattices, heterojunctive
Graphed from the air, your cropmarked farmlands
Are epitaxies of tweed.

All night motorways carry your signal, swept
To East Kilbride or Dunfermline. A brightness off low
    headlands
Beams-in the dawn to Fife's interstices,
Optoelectronics of hay.

Micro-nation. So small you cannot be forgotten,
Bible inscribed on a ricegrain, hi-tech's key
Locked into the earth, your televised Glasgows
Are broadcast in Rio. Among circuitboard crowsteps

To be miniaturised is not small-minded.
To love you needs more details than the Book of Kells –
Your harbours, your photography, your democratic intellect
Still boundless, chip of a nation.

A Scottish Assembly

Circuitry's electronic tartan, the sea,
Libraries, fields – I want the lot

To fly off and scatter, but most of all
Always to come home to roost

In this unkempt country where a handicapped printer,
Engraver of dog collars, began with his friends

The ultimate encyclopedia.
Don't expect any rhyme or reason

For Scotland remaining an explosion reversed
Or ordinariness a fruited vine

Or why I came back here to choose my union
On the side of the ayes, remaining a part

Of this diverse assembly – Benbecula, Glasgow, Bow of
    Fife –
Voting with my feet, and this hand.

John Logie Baird

When it rained past Dumbarton Rock
You skipped Classics for a motorbike exploration

Of the Clyde's slow Raj. In sodden memsahibs' gardens
Hydrangeas unfurled into fibre-optics.

A dominie lochgellied you once
For pronouncing 'Eelensburgh' like those wild, untouchable
    tinks

Who, if they could see your biker's career from today's
Long distance, would snigger. A socialist most famous for

Inventing an undersock, screened from douce cousins,
Under bamboos at a small jam factory

Near Port of Spain you achieved television
And paid for it. At the trials a boy called Reith

Risen from your old class shook hands, then wrote you off.
You worked. When World War II ended

Baird equipment broadcast victory in the Savoy
But not one diner said cheerio when you faded,

An obsolete wallah, edited out, still beaming
One hand outstretched across those Clydelike waves.

Alba Einstein

When proof of Einstein's Glaswegian birth
First hit the media everything else was dropped:
Logie Baird, Dundee painters, David Hume – all
Got the big E. Physics documentaries
Became peak-viewing; Scots publishers hurled awa
MacDiarmid like an overbaked potato, and swooped
On the memorabilia: *Einstein Used My Fruitshop,*
Einstein in Old Postcards, Einstein's Bearsden Relatives.
Hot on their heels came the A. E. Fun Park,
Quantum Court, Glen Einstein Highland Malt.
Glasgow was booming. Scotland rose to its feet
At Albert Suppers where The Toast to the General Theory
Was given by footballers, panto-dames, or restaurateurs.
In the US an ageing lab-technician recorded
How the Great Man when excited showed a telltale glottal
    stop.
He'd loved fiddlers' rallies. His favourite sport was curling.
Thanks to this, Scottish business expanded
Endlessly. His head grew toby-jug-shaped,
Ideal for keyrings. He'd always worn brogues.
Ate bannocks in exile. As a wee boy he'd read *The Beano.*
His name brought new energy: our culture was solidly based
On pride in our hero, The Universal Scot.

Fur Thi Muse o Synthesis

Interkat intercommuner, intercommunin
At aw leid's interfaces, skeich
Tae interpone a hooch that intermells
An interverts auld jorrams tae reconduct
Aureat thru lingua franca, intercommoun
Thru joie-de-vivre-wurds, guttir thru dictionar, it's
yirsel's
Thi ane I T, thi richt wurdbank, fettle
Thru thi hert's printoot, wi'oot figmalirie tae spairge
Or jevel thi speerit. Interclosin delicht,
Wulcat dotmatrixed fur aye fae Jamieson
Lik a delicut pomerie oar thi epitaxy layerin
Crystals wi a pink o molecular beam, yi kythe hirdum
dirdum
Tae gowks, mebbe, but yi've a gledge o beauty
That'll magnetize lummles, an yir lusbirdans o
phonemes hae sprent
Tae staun oan thi mune, tae ratch licht fae skau, an tae
sacre
Fowk vivual an vieve again whan thi makars wha cam
Tae thi keyburd o thi leid lik piper's invites
Richt-furthe find it an interteneyare that maks
Regenerate thi stolum o Scoatlan.

Intricate negotiator between factions at variance, having intercourse at all language's interfaces, apt to startlingly interpose a cry of joy that intermingles and appropriates to a new, unfamiliar use old slow, melancholy boatsongs to reconduct high diction through common speech, the language of conversation through exclamations of delight, gutter through dictionary, it's you who are the only Information Technology, the true word-bank, speech-energy through the heart's printout, without whim to spatter or joggle the spirit. Intercepting delight, wildcat dotmatrixed forever from Jamieson's *Dictionary of the Scottish Language* like a delicate orchard or the epitaxy layering crystals with a perfect glitter of molecular beam, you appear confused nonsense to fools, maybe, but you have an oblique look of beauty that will magnetize metal filings, and your pygmies of phonemes have leapt to stand on the moon, to dislocate light from total ruin, and to consecrate people alive and lively again when the poets who came to the keyboard of the language as if they were the last folk to be invited to a party immediately discover it to be an entertainer of guests which makes regenerate the large, broken off fragment of Scotland.

Ghetto-Blastir

Ghetto-makars, tae the knackirs'
Wi aw yir schemes, yir smug dour dreams
O yir ain feet. Yi're beat
By yon new Scoatlan loupin tae yir street

Wi a Jarre-lik puissance, ghetto-blastin
Auld sangs crooned doon
Yir reedy beaks, wastin an tastin
O deid pus. See us? We're foon

Wi whit's new, wi aw that's speerin oot
An cummin hame tae roost, tae set the feathirs
Flyin in yir kailyard. Scoot
Tae yir hales, tak tae yir heels, blethirs,

Wee naethins aye feathrin yir ain nests
O douce semis! Yir psychadelic tartan's
Shite tae oor white nichts an aw the guests
Oor laughtir's aftir. Sook yir fozie cartons

O guttir music, mak the Muse seik uttir-
lie wi yir gabbin, stabbin, sabbin
Ochones. Gang tae the Gents' an muttir.
Ladies tae! Bicoz we're grabbin

Whit's left o the leid tae mak anither sang
O semiconducters, Clydes aw dancin fastir
Than yir feart shanks. Ye'll scraich tae hear amang
Pooer-clubs an cliques, twee pubs o freaks,
When cockiedoodlin doon yir beaks

The raucus sweet soon o oor Ghetto-Blastir.

*Ochones – lamenting noise made by a Lowlander when imitating
Gaelic speech; scraich – cry like an alarmed hen.*

Prayer

Upstream from shattered urban lintels
Lost crofts are soft as new bread.

That dripping tap in the one-walled kitchen
Reminds someone there will be a need
Of water before and after.

Sin to imagine a perfect world
Without embarrassment, rain, or prayer.
A hand is clasping my other hand

In a dark place that has to be got through
On a wing and. Listen to this.

David Kinloch

David Kinloch

‘ I was born in Glasgow in 1959 and was educated there, graduating from Glasgow University in 1982. From then until 1990, when I returned to Glasgow, I travelled around a bit, studying and teaching French in a variety of places, including Oxford, Paris, Swansea and Manchester. It was only after leaving Glasgow that I realised how important Scotland was to me and that I wanted to return.

One of my principal interests at the moment is in creating relatively large-scale structures which allow different kinds of poetry to counterpoint each other. What happens when 'traditional' musical (the music is very important) lyrics cohabit with more experimental prose poems and fables? This idea is central to *Dustie-Fute* which is the first part of a poem in three sections. In this poem, the old Scots word for a troubadour or jongleur, juggler or merchant, jumps out of Jamieson's Dictionary and, rather like Orpheus, sails off on the Renfrew Ferry into an Underworld of secret or suppressed languages. *Dustie-Fute*, however is not a poem about old words, nor is it simply a poem about the difficulty for many writers of my generation who would like to write in Scots more fluently than they are able. These unexpected, boisterous words become in the course of the poem a kind of metaphor for the queer and wonderful tongue that is dying prematurely in the mouths of young men killed off by Aids.

What is it like to live and to die as a gay man in Scotland in the 1990's? What is it like to be in love, to be responsible and find that love and responsibility dishonoured by many who surround you? What is it like to want to write a poetry that orchestrates a range of competing voices and textures in the belief that only in this way can you do justice to the complex emotions and ideas such questions provoke? These are some of the questions my poems are trying to ask. ’

Publications:

Poems in *Other Tongues* (Verse, 1990); *Dustie-Fute* (Vennel Press, 1992); *The Thought and Art of Joseph Joubert* (OUP, 1992); *Reading Douglas Dunn* (co-editor with Robert Crawford, EUP, 1992).

The Rev. Robert Walker Skating on Duddingston Loch

The water tensed at his instruction
and trout gazed up at his incisive feet.
We felt that God must be in clarity like this
and listened to the dull glens echo
the striations of his silver blades.

Far out on Duddingston loch
our true apostle sped
with twice the speed of Christ
who walked on waves.

We saw him harrow ice
with grace of the elect
and scar the transubstantiation
of wintered elements.

With a sense of real presence
he crossed our loch
what need of vestments
with such elegant legs?

Dustie-Fute

When I opened my window and reached for the yoghurt cooling on the outside ledge, it had gone. All that remained was a single Scottish word bewildered by the Paris winter frost and the lights of its riverbank motorways. What can *dustie-fute* have to say to a night like this? How can it dangle on its hyphen down into the rue Geoffrey L'Asnier where Danton stayed on the eve of revolution? How can it tame this strangeness for me or change me into the cupolas and flagstones I so desire yet still notice every time I walk among them? Does the 'auld alliance' of words and things stand a chance among the traffic and pimps in the Publicis Saint-Germain? For it's not as if *dustie-fute* were my familiar. I could easily confuse *dustie-fute* with *elfmill* which is the sound made by a worm in the timber of a house, supposed by the vulgar to be preternatural. These words are as foreign as the city they have parachuted into, dead words slipping on the sill of a living metropolis. They are extremes that touch like dangerous wires and the only hope for them, for us, is the space they inhabit, a room Cioran speaks of, veering between dilettantism and dynamite. Old Scots word, big French city and in between abysmal me: ane merchand or creamer, quha hes no certain dwelling place, quhair the dust may be dicht fra hes feete or schone. Dustie-fute, a stranger, equivalent to *fairand-man*, at a loss in the empty soul of his ancestors' beautiful language and in the soulless city of his compeers living the 21st century now and scoffing at his medieval wares. Yet here, precisely here, is their rendez-vous and triumphantly, stuffed down his sock, an oblique sense, the dustie-fute of 'revelry', the acrobat, the juggler who accompanies the toe-belled jongleur with his merchant's comic fairground face. He reaches deep into his base latinity, into his *pede-pulverosi* and French descendants pull out their own *pieds poudreux*. Dustie-fute remembers previous lives amid the plate glass of Les Halles. They magnify his motley, his mid-oranges, his hawker lyrics and for a second Beaubourg words graze Scottish glass then glance apart. In this revelry differences copulate, become more visible and bearable and, stranger than the words or city I inhabit, I reach for my yoghurt and find it there.

The Love That Dare Not

Even the illness that extinguishes it comes in borrowed clothes, not one name but many, forming the syntax of your end. Unravelling its hidden meanings, side-stepping tears that dare not fall yet because they would admit the last page of this dictionary has been turned, I trace you back, nudging you, as I used to, from word to word:

the days you called me *rinker*, a tall, thin, long-legged horse, a bloody harridan, I called you *rintherout*, a gadabout, a needy, homeless vagrant, like the tongue we spoke beneath the sheets. Our life as mobile and happy as the half a dozen Scottish verbs I'd push across a page on Sunday afternoons, trying to select a single meaning.

Here it is: under *Ripple* or *Rippill*, a squat paragraph which tells us we must separate the seed of flax from the stalk, undo our badly-done work, separate and tear in pieces. And when we are birds, must eat grains of standing corn, when clouds, open up, disperse, clear off. Its noun has you in its grip: an instrument with teeth for rippling flax.

Or you might find us under *set* which seats, places hens on eggs in order to hatch them, assigns work, settles, gets in order; puts milk into a pan for the cream to rise, sets fishing-lines or nets, works according to a pattern, plants potatoes, makes, impels, includes, besets, brings to a halt and puzzles, nauseates, disgusts, marks game, lets, leases, sends, dispatches, becomes, suits, beseems, sits, ceases to grow, becomes mature, stiffens, congeals, starts, begins, sets off

The love that dare not Except that now, so near the end, when I would like to hold you and have been forbidden, I search for it in your eyes, daring their definition.

The Clinic

The clinic records false names,
Assigns us leaflets and a Sister
Who calls us 'boys'. A doctor,
Briefly green and ponderous,
Assumes that 'friend' from my tongue
Is a euphemism, and poises pen
Above white boxes for supplementary
Non-grata. We are not here

Imagining instead a big breezy
Bed on Kingsbarns beach,
No need for bandages on hands
Where eczema leaves tiny pits
For love's curious virus.

No sweat. It is safe inside him,

Sealed by skin against sun and water,
A hermit cell among the cells
Which one day will strike out
From shore and evangelize.

Envoi: Warmer Bruder

(a slang expression for homosexual, literally, 'hot brother'. It gave rise to many vicious puns in concentration camps like Sachsenhausen and Flossenburg.)

i

Concentrate hot brothers:
Shovel snow with me
In Sachsenhausen
From one side to the other
And back again.

Then in the silence
Make an angel of the snow
Which falls unceasingly
On camp and foe.

The lights of Grangemouth
Dance their triangles
Into tears,
Its smoke the ghost of blood,
The melting snow.

ii

Concentrate hot brothers:
Make an angel of the snow
And shovel Sachsenhausen
Silence from one side to the other
And back again.

O warmer bruder
Tonight you fall
Shaping car windows
With triangles of Grangemouth light.

Smoke, the ghost of blood,
Fills up the melting sky.

iii

Blood dropped on Sachsenhausen
Snow was silenced,
Shovelled out of history.
But here in Scotland
It does not melt

And cloaks the Grangemouth
Sky with red triangles.
This is no sunset
But concentrated smoke
That stings the eye.

iv

Triangles of smoke
Blood the Grangemouth skies.
Along the Forth the hospice
Workers shovel snow

From drives that keep the patients
Bound, while silence, like an angel,
Visits and stays on.

The Tear in Pat Kane's Voice

The tear in Pat Kane's voice
Offers you the shadow of a bi-plane
Unutterably high just next to silence:

Off the grain, it thinks more quickly
Than the images of his songs
And each true thought concludes
In the break where each true note begins.

The tear in Pat Kane's voice
Offers you a man's name,
Whiter and harder than Alba:

Adorno at his plain table,
Rubbing out the barbaric lyrics
Of post-Auschwitz poets

And cleansed children,
Desperately seeking a river crossing
In a blown-up ferry,
While we sit like empty cars
In a reconverted bauble,
Crossing from one song to
Another over the nailed-down waves.

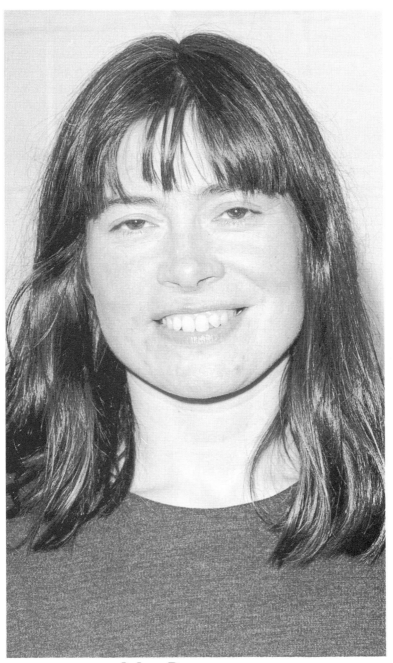

Meg Bateman

❛ I was born in Edinburgh in 1959 of English parents. The household was very cheery, with family friends constantly dropping in and a lot of talk. My father in particular loved life. I went to Aberdeen University to study Celtic, and spent a lot of time in the Islands, very conscious that part of that subject's attraction for me was that it was such a different world from the milieu of my upbringing. After graduating I did a PhD about medieval Gaelic religious poetry, and have since then been teaching Gaelic, first in Edinburgh and now at Aberdeen University.

When I was about 23 I experienced some events in love and in the family that made me feel an end had come to happiness and the sort of innocence I had known hitherto. It is not the sort of thing you can discuss, so I started to write for the first time, and in Gaelic. I wrote in Gaelic partly for secrecy, partly because having done a degree in it I knew about it, but mostly because it was through my reading of Gaelic song-poetry that I had developed a notion of the sort of poetry I wanted to create myself. I did not want to produce confessional or idiosyncratic, or even original, poetry; rather I wanted it to have a sort of leanness, an inevitability about it, both formally and emotionally. Of the poems printed here, *Aotramachd* perhaps comes nearest to this ideal of mine.

I do not like to read my poems anymore. They belong to a specific time in my life when I felt my response to the demands of love to be humiliatingly inadequate. Since then I have grown pragmatic and in consequence have written virtually nothing in the last four years. I do however remember the excitement and the absorption of all my best effort that poetry-writing entailed. ❜

Publications:

Orain Ghaoil/Amhráin Ghrá (Coiscéim, 1990)

Some of my poems appear in the following anthologies:

Fresh Oceans, (Stramullion, 1988)
Other Tongues (Verse, 1990)
Twenty of the Best (Galliard, 1990)

An Aghaidh na Siorraidheachd/In the Face of Eternity (Polygon, 1991)
Internal Landscapes (America, 1992)
Sruth na Maoile (Canongate, 1993)

My translations of Gaelic poetry into English appear in:

An Anthology of Scottish Women Poets (EUP, 1991)
The Harp's Cry (Birlinn, 1993)

A chionn 's gu robh mi measail air

Thigeadh e thugam
nuair a bha e air mhisg
   a chionn 's gu robh mi measail air.

Dhèanainn ti dha
is dh'èisdinn ris
   a chionn 's gu robh mi measail air.

Sguir e a dh'òl
is rinn mi gàirdeachas leis
   a chionn 's gu robh mi measail air.

Nist cha tig e tuilleadh
is nì e tàir orm
   a chionn 's gu robh mi measail air.

Because I was so fond of him

He used to come to me
when he was drunk
    because I was so fond of him.

I'd make him tea
and listen to him
    because I was so fond of him.

He stopped drinking
and I was pleased for him
    because I was so fond of him.

Now he comes no more,
indeed he despises me,
    because I was so fond of him.

Garradh Moray Place, an Dùn Eideann

Duilleagan dubha air an fheur,
fàileadh searbh na cloiche taise,
sop odhar de cheò
ga ìsleachadh mu na craobhan;
a' coimhead a-mach à bròn,
mòr-shùilean m' athar,
duilleag a' snìomh gu làr –
gluasad m' aigne.

Mun cuairt, coire thaighean drùidhteach,
comharra aois glòir-mhiannaich,
òrduighean cholbh clasaigeach
nach aithnich laigse san duine.

Gàrradh tathaichte aig bantraichean
fàilligeach, neo-eisimeileach,
a' coiseachd ann an cianalas an làithean,
an uallaichean ceilte.

Ach cluinnear an seo gliongartaich
coilearan chon grinn-cheumnach,
is chithear, fa chomhair nan taighean,
meanbh-dhuilleagan soilleir
gan leigeil sìos gu sèimh
aig a' bheithe chiùin, chuimir.

Moray Place Gardens, Edinburgh

Black leaves on the grass,
an acrid smell of damp stonework,
a wisp of ochre fog
lowering itself around the trees,
looking out from sorrow
my father's great eyes,
a leaf spinning to the ground –
the motion of my spirits.

All round, a cauldron of imposing houses,
sign of an ambitious age,
orders of classical columns
that do not countenance human frailty.

Gardens haunted by widows,
failing, independent,
walking in the wearisomeness of their days,
their burdens concealed.

But tinkling is heard here
from the collars of neatly-stepping dogs,
and against the houses
tiny bright leaves are seen
with the shapely birch tree
gently letting them go.

Alba fo Dhìmeas

Chuala mi oileanach ag ràdh,
'Luchd nan eilean, chan iongantach
gur suarach an cultar –
dè 'n cothrom a th'aca air ealain?'

Is lean fear eile air,
'Mura biodh an t-Ath-Leasachadh,
bhitheadh Mozart is Verdi
againn fhìn ann an Alba . . .'

Tha mi ag ionnsachadh bhuapa
gu bheil obair an oideachais coilionta;
a-nist chan fhaic iad
an grinneas nan dualchas.

Sioladh na Gàidhlig

Thug thu tuigse dham inntinn
air sìoladh rud nach till a leithid,
air creachadh air a' chinne-daonna
nach gabh leasachadh . . .

Cailleach air bàsachadh aig baile,
ròpa t' acaire a' caitheamh;
nist tha mi a' faicinn nad shùilean
briseadh-cridhe na cùise

Scotland Despised

I heard a student say,
'The teuchters, it's not surprising
their culture's pathetic;
what chance have they to see the arts?'

And another continued,
'But for the Reformation
we'd have a Mozart and a Verdi
of our own in Scotland . . .'

I'm learning from them
the business of education is complete,
now they will not see
the fineness in their heritage.

The loss of Gaelic

You gave me an intellectual grasp
of something unique dying out,
of a despoiling of humanity
for which there can be no reparation . . .

An old woman dies at home,
your anchor rope is fraying;
now I can see in your eyes
the heart-break of the matter.

Aotromachd

B'e t' aotromachd a rinn mo thàladh,
aotromachd do chainnte 's do ghàire,
aotromachd do lethchinn nam làmhan,
t' aotromachd lurach ùr mhàlda;
agus 's e aotromachd do phòige
tha a' cur trasg air mo bheòil-sa,
's 's e aotromachd do ghlaic mum chuairt-sa
a leigeas leis an t-sruth mi.

Gille a' Sireadh Obair

Duilleag bhàn-bhuidhe
  a' tionndadh air a faillean 's a' tèarnadh,
a' fàs nas lugha, nas rèidhe,
mar t' aodann an-diugh
aig *roundabouts* is *slipways*
air na rathaidean gu deas,
a' sleamhnachadh bhuam
sìos ioma-shlighe m' aineoil.

Agus fhathast laigh thu nam ghàirdeanan
fad na h-oidhche raoir,
's dh'fhàg do chruinnead ghrinn òg
a lorg air mo bhoisean,
gam phianadh leis a' chùram
a bha air Eubha mu Adhamh,
mise, boireannach gun ainm,
's tusa, gille bho thuath.

Lightness

It was your lightness that drew me,
the lightness of your talk and your laughter,
the lightness of your cheek in my hands,
your sweet gentle modest lightness;
and it is the lightness of your kiss
that is starving my mouth,
and the lightness of your embrace
that will let me go adrift.

Boy Looking for Work

A pale-yellow leaf
turning on its twig and dropping,
growing smaller, flatter
like your face today
at roundabouts and slipways
on the motorways south,
sliding away from me
down a labyrinth of difference.

And yet last night you lay in my arms
all night long,
and your neat young roundness
left its imprint on my palms,
hurting me with the tenderness
Eve knew for Adam,
me, an anonymous woman,
and you, a boy from the North.

Leigeil Bhruadairean Dhìom

Tha am feasgar ciùin,
an t-adhar san uinneig
gun smàl . . .
Isd, m' eudail,
na bruidhinn an dràsd,
tha taibhsean a'dol siar.

Chan e fear àraidh a chaoininn
ach beatha de mhiann,
gach roghainn neo-thaghte
gam threigsinn
air do shàileabh, fhir bhàin.

Dèan caithris leam
gus an tèid iad à sealladh.
Cha tig iad nar dàil, oir
is euchdaiche na iad
do shìol nam bhroinn, is dèine
bhios gul ar ciad-ghin
nuair a thogas tu e os àird.

A Letting Go of Dreams

The evening is calm,
the sky in the window
without stain . . .
Hush, my love,
don't talk now –
ghosts are going by.

No one man do I mourn
but a life-time's longing,
every unmade choice
slipping from me
because of you, fair man.

Watch with me
till they are out of sight.
They will not hurt us, for
more potent than they
your seed in my womb, keener
the cry of our firstborn
when you raise it up on high.

Iain Bamforth

❛ My father (English) and my mother (Scottish) met, symboli-
cally enough, on holiday in the Borders where my father was on
National Service leave and my mother was finishing her MA. I
was born, the first of four children, in 1959, in Bishop's Stortford,
but my parents soon moved to Glasgow where I grew up on the
south side, graduating in medicine from the University in 1982.

My childhood was out-of-date even before I'd lived it. Our
house resonated to the rhythms of the Old Testament, and it
wouldn't be an exaggeration to say that the 'worldliest' books in
the house (no television, no radio) were the *Collected Works of
Scott*. Both my parents (and nearly all my relatives, except the
ones who got away) were Plymouth, or Exclusive Brethren, a
smallish fundamentalist group which was founded in the last
great religious revival to sweep the British Isles, in 1838. My early
consciousness is stamped with two facts: the imminent return of
Christ, and being told I was 'saved' (i.e. I wasn't supposed to
worry about the first). Fear and dread (and crude psychological
techniques) hooped people together in what was to become an
increasingly Americanized cult (it broke apart under the weight
of its own contradictions in 1970); but given its strangely subver-
sive nature (though the Brethren wouldn't have thought so) I find
it difficult to account for my own poetry without worrying away
at the nodes between radical politics and religious dissent. Ex-
pecting the End-Time any time gives the imaginative life purpose
and intensity, albeit of the narrowest kind.

Medicine likes to think it's a hyperrational, universal culture.
It's neither, but few places in the world are closed to someone
with a medical degree. I've been able to practise medicine in Paris,
Bavaria and the Australian outback, as well as in Scotland, and
write poetry in the gaps. I've worked too as a scientific translator,
and find myself impatient to open my poetry to the conventionally
'non-poetic', to indeterminacy and process, since poetry seems to
me, not least in its attitude to the self, still assiduously Romantic.
What keeps me on the move is a sense that difference is a vital
element for me, like an anthropologist who goes on a field-trip
to find on returning that he has been irremediably changed by the
'observation'.

Escape from history unites my religious upbringing and the
deep dreams of Scotland, and I'm suspicious about the absolute

need for redemption which has blasted both. Scots words step quite familiarly into my poems, since they fit my accent, or because they're couthy. I admit to occasional dictionary-trawling. Speaking a language stripped of its diction has made us absurdly politicized and defensive; rather than take the history of Scotland as a dream-pathology of social embarrassment or historical belatedness, my poems usually start from the premiss that those discontinuities, time-lapses and demons are what has made us modern. **)**

Publications:

The Modern Copernicus (Salamander Press, 1984)
Sons and Pioneers (Carcanet, 1992)

Men on Fire

Being a land of dissent and magnificent defeats
it evolved a subtle theology of failure, stealing its own thunder
wherever two or three were gathered together
and the occult plumbing groaned querulously beneath the boards.

These days, it grows owlish with hindsight –
recounting itself as a salvo of rain far north on mappamundi,
who's who of a supernumerary Creation myth
that swallowed the serpent's tail, ate the offspring whole.

When Rousseau exhumed the weather over Waverley
its civil imaginary became a fast diminishing return.
Few Encyclopaedists recall the genealogy backpacked out of Troy
or the vernacular of a silver-tongued Golden Age.

Later it saw itself arsy-versy, a nation after the letter;
but common cause outreaching the Dutch
it sold its birthright for a cut of the glory . . .
a mere idea, it seemed invincible.

Yet it thrived on its own lost cause, and the mark of Cain
was a lefthandedness it practised righteously –
its sentinel cities on the plain a gritty paradigm
for an industry of calloused hands.

Guilt was one thing it exported to the new world;
ballast to the quantum energy ascending through midnight suns
as a monument of candour, men on fire:
here, in the old, sorrow recurs as a brief downpour,

dream-fug, supplements to a Journal of the Plague Year
when the gospel of virtues, that manic uprightness,
laid blame at nobody's door but its own . . .
beyond reach of heaven was a legislature pining for hell.

Out of it, sons and daughters have no clear sighting
of how an apple-tree opens the debate
but know it does, since they find themselves

on a mission without a motor, reciting the plot backwards

while pavements become rain-sleeked and lustral
and an oddly buoyant cargo gospel
swims through anti-matter to the hard edge of the landscape.
Like a native technology, it starts from what's left

and salvages its own future, a startled Doric narrative
stalking the wet track, tongue and tinder
to its radical children, shy to touch the incontrovertible ores
of a faith that has lately outgrown its disappointment.

Calvinist Geography

– A northern supremacist monad!
It eavesdrops, shrewd dissertation:
goes out to shoot converts
when light drips through the roof
and the day leans to, a gob
of consternation at the easy drama

of the dark. Novel as any nation
it grows on you like a fuggy absence,
archaic body, story's end.
What's left limps back to first
causes, the old betrayals –
though no one's wiser now

the fire's smoored and a soft smirr
drifts in across the moors. *Or
it blows wrong, a chill family epic
kept wrapped for redemption:
when the renegade sermons start up
again, from clumps of rock*

*and scraggy deserts between estates,
they tell you more than you want
to know about persistence*

and extinction, the risen towns
gravid with herring, crazed fiddlers
making a palaver in the square –

or here on one of Wade's roads
where the servile myths skite home
to sour news, the barracking
of a threadbare ruinous country.
It holds an accent out, in self-defence.
Sweet as failure, you can taste

feral voices on the tongue:
success, they say, will always
ring a hollow change, like sorrow.
Attrition, diaspora: they're children
from an illfitting marriage;
shipped off to weather continents

without a say-so in the sublimations
of unreadiness. Trite tradition,
it leaves its interpreters
stuck on voes, shouting across islands
for the pure light of justice.
Underfoot, it's the usual unison,

granite voices thinking they're already
home, though the sun could tell
why happiness is hostile. Hard
breathing, flight's nervous feathers,
always get goosed. *Wind scolds*
like a mother, and soon the moon

has pale ideas of its own, none new
to the narrator. Names are maps
among the oxbows and civic drumlins;
open secrets. They inhale
suprise, subtilized by circumstance,
a blunt determination to make good

that could easily spend another century
riddling for old catastrophes,

cleared spaces, idylls, odd ideals.
There's no new peak, hardly even
a pent Sunday or an underground edition.
Irony's a glib surface like the sea:

a spit of land, a cold promontory
where goodness has to be spat on too
when the day's done. *No thought*
of comfort or compensation:
the joke about deserters wasn't one.
Work it out, then: either rescue it

from its talk of beginnings or know
you might be right, being wrong.
It drives off through rain
and conflagrations, in all directions,
passes proof to the snug compass.
Now it's dark it's almost dawn.

Alibis

It was a barely perceptible affront.
Mr Wordly Wiseman took sentimental fright
in the arms of a carnival victim who spoke no English
and a bulemic variety of the patios . . .
métro, boulot, dodo of an hexagonal affair.

Beneath my window, the Street of the Dry Tree
led down to the Pont Neuf: new to the *ancien régime*
and still new to a discredited 18th Brumaire –
those bourgeois sins, complacency and self-regard,
strode out of their century, asking why we needed this . . .

The other side, past the eviscerated belly of Paris,
was a tour through the skin trade: fast food, fast sex
and a gallic Punch giving Judy the once-over;
little secrets Maigret might have kept from his wife
and the big-time vendors of the naked truth.

By the door, I'd stacked the empties, my cadavers.
I was reading Brecht on the hell of the disenchanters
and watching my deaf-dumb neighbour watching me . . .
Twice weekly to buy milk, and long afternoon surveillances
till the pigeons hauled the daylight home.

Every evening, I drowsed to an upstairs *Liebestod.*
Someone was dreaming of being a frontiersman in America
or stalking Flaubert to the lower reaches of the Nile:
watermarks on the wall of the local morgue.
Tracking sun-spots, I compounded my dream-interest.

I was glossing the storyline as fast as I dared
in a place my grandpa called Babylon, the Antichrist *chez lui.*
Deaf to domesdays, it was still crossing itself
or chafing the epochs like a cod-accordion . . .
scraping by on Piaf-naif dreams of glory.

To the silent majority this was never the End-of-Days.
In Figaro's marriage, their namesakes had forced the hand;
centuries later they were still living off the dowry . . .
That retro-radical flight from history
was the snore of the old world outliving itself.

Before the continental drift of two wars
I could imagine Nerval trailing home his livid lobster
to a draughty grammar and the past's Latin drone.
After Haussmann, every lamppost was an orator
interrogating the breezy dispersal of the Communards.

Candid, the swans hissed from the oil-slicked Seine
and made me a duvet beneath the rafters.
After the rest went south one always stayed behind,
its head beneath its wing, flim-flamming the current;
undemocratic, a hesitant Belgian joke.

Halfheartedly I studied the semiotics of couscous
or watched the French devour their colonies.
I bore my life to the Deux Magots and left the ashes there;
a diagram of detours, another unfinished novel.
I took a visceral interest in my precarious species.

Curdled leftovers occluded the windowsill.
Whatever they meant was there to keep me in my place
till the damp became a sticky resurrection.
In one myth of the private life I was killing time
even I joined them in exhaustion, passion's last logic.

Better to play the medicine man, overhauling the rich
with pop-Oedipal recipes out of Dr Pangloss.
I listened to the histories of hundreds of bodies,
anaesthetic, *involontaire*, subsumed in the mesmeric aura
of everlasting life, an odd entropic metaphor.

Back came the comic echo, news of my four bare walls . . .
I was a novice, fingering the sacramental relics,
eaten whole by the culture fetishists.
Satisfaction was the gape-mouthed, cruel, pacific god
who gave me everything, even the need itself.

And art or absinthe a way of swamping Giant Despair!
Faute de mieux, I made a virtue of my contradictions –
humour was the one weapon to unseat the era.
But when I started hearing panic behind the mockery
the joke had come too close to home.

Tomtoms drummed me back at night from the Big Arch –
Speer's neo-geo paradigm, marmoreal in white Carrara –
to a counter-city in the galleries at Châtelet.
I took the pons asinorum to maturity,
chose a destiny, lit up, went back to my subterfuge.

Beside me, in the next block, lived the ultimate collector.
I never saw him, only heard the poisoned whisperings:
one day they called the *pompiers* in to clean him out,
houseproud among a decade's scatological relics,
each one labelled, wrapped and catalogued.

Rain Diary

You hardly have to say the word and it's here, hauling
Banff Bailiffs across the streets of Europe
to one of Joyce's reclaimed 'funams of waste arenary soil',
Nora breathing 'O Jim!' the very day he stopped
in the Bleibtreustrasse and watched it pour down flights,
his nation's *esprit de l'escalier*. Reading it
is like explaining a heresy, its one-offs and torrents
soodling, dropwise, sklent notations of delight.
It takes women of the sun cultures indoors, fingers
in every recess. Damp clothes drop like names
in the rue du Cherche-Midi, soft exclamations
and no talk of respite, only poor men and pike staves.
Half an hour later, like Mercutio, it recalls them
to the ordinary. Beyond the comic the credible;
but that was before it had gone a while down-under
and swept a town off its feet. It disappears inside itself
like an enharmonic pun; its iron cataracts yielding
a blue moon to the platitudes of assent
blowing upwards sheer off mountains. Vigil levels out
in its aftermath. It mists futures, pocks stone
with slow acids, leaving no one outside
dragging neighbours to his wake while the moon
slumps in the midden. Some keep it in clay pots, hoping
a flaff will dry it on the change or temper
the peaty spirit, its sublimation of the very worst.
Like Vico's history, it's a spatial form of coming back;
rigorously errant, faithful to its origins.
Hospitality grows from watersigns, its toponymic limbo.
Undemonstrative, it dumps chill messages,
finds lovers everywhere, scuffing down from saga-steads
like serendipity, striking out the excursus
it once made to an attentive rapt face on the watergaw
fixed half a childhood over the Broomielaw. Our pluvial towns
step out of history, and watch themselves get wet.

Margaret Fulton Cook

Graham Fulton

Graham Fulton

❛ I was born in 1959. I went to school and left school. I went to Art college and left Art college. Since then I've worked in a number of places culminating in the one I'm in just now. I live in Paisley.

The way it is. Ordinary people doing ordinary things. But what we take for granted, if looked at long enough from a different angle, can become funny, bizarre, claustrophobic or frightening. Normal behaviour is all around us. The humdrum is the source of poetry. That's what I try to capture on sheets of white paper.

Some of the poems seem as if they've been dipped in cynicism. Probably so. It's a dangerous place out there. Hopefully there's enough humour and concern, alongside the stuff coughed up by old uncle subconscious, to balance the picture. There's a thin line between comedy and tragedy, madness and sanity, ugliness and beauty. It's all interchangeable. I've got no gasp-inducing message to ram down unsuspecting throats. I just report on what's going on as seen through my eyes. What else is there but what we remember and what we see now. Tiny incidents pounced on years later can have a resonance and significance that wasn't apparent at the time. Tiny clues to something or other. Sometimes the landscape can change from Scotland to Paris or New York or wherever, but it's all the same. People are at the centre of all the poems. People trying to find a kind of dignity. People left behind on the lower floors.

I've learnt from a small pool of poets, all separated by decades and distance but all unified in their celebration of the astonishing world of the ordinary as well as their attitude and approach to writing. Find your own rhythms and vocabulary and say what you see as truthfully as you can. Anything can be written about. It's all waiting. Nothing is unimportant or taboo. It's just a question of really seeing what's always been there in front of your face. ❜

Publications:

Tower of Babble (with Bobby Christie, Ronald McNeil and Jim Ferguson) (Itinerant, 1987)
The Eighth Dwarf (Itinerant, 1989)

Humouring the Iron Bar Man (Polygon, 1990)
This (Rebel Inc. Publications, 1993)

forthcoming
Knights of the Lower Floors (Polygon, 1994)

Charles Manson Auditions for the Monkees

'We're just trying
              to be friendly'
he sings to the suits
              who make
the choice.
A truly groovy
           American boy.
Dolenz!
      Polanski!
            Underage sex!
An X
    for outcast
between his eyes,
             a guitar
slung across
        his back.
Charlie wants
        to be an Axe-hero,
Charlie has mastered
            tricky chord changes,
Charlie has memorised lines
                that
the Beatles haven't written
              yet.
He knows about
           Rickenbackers,
knows about
        Revelations,
knows he didn't
          get much
education,
       knows
he hasn't
    a hope
in hell.
He should invest
         in a pom-pom hat,
swap his uniform

for another
loveable grin,
puddingbowl trim.
Nesmith!
LaBianca!
Tork!
A man
with murder
in his heart
is not what they want
in a primetime slot,
not what's required
for the ratings
war,
not what they need
for the decade
of flowers.
He hasn't
grown
a beard
so far.
He thinks
"There's
plenty of time
to tell my girls
to lift their knives
and make their mark,
sneakout and freakout
in Beverly Hills,
shoot the high-school creeps
in the head,
slice the starlets
with babies inside them,
be the American monster
that Americans
like their monsters
to be.
San Quentin!
Piggies!
Sharon Tate!
Let the powermen

                    see my face
          on the cover of
                    LIFE Magazine,
          let them all
                    be believers,
          let them be
                    in love
          with my version of
                    The American dream
          as they taste their
                              root
          beers,
                    as they bite
          their cookies
                              but
          till then I'll sing
                    my saddest song,
          let the judges know
                              'We get the funniest looks
          from
                    everyone we meet –
          Hey! Hey! . . . .'

The Unmasking Scene

Tinted purple and
          in synchronisation
with an upright piano

          Mary Philbin unmasked

Lon Chaney

          to reveal a wire
trussed nose and
          a receding hairline

which were essential

credentials for an

artist in the Twenties
            until my mantis baby
with varnished toenails

            gave me her halo to stop me

growing out of my trousers

            and asked me where it
all went wrong
            to which I offered

'Spineless and spiteful or

            something or other'

and she gave me her popcorn
            to stop my tummy rumbling
and I enquired what

            I required to be an
artist in the Eighties

            for I realised she had
an answer to everything
            and she replied with a sigh

'A vicious streak is

            fine and dandy

a fucked-up life can
            come in handy'
and she searched for her toothbrush

            to help flush the dreaming

while I sent postcards

> to my brylcreem friends
> until the leeches
> were delivered and
>
> Lon disappeared
>
> beneath the Seine

Humouring the Iron Bar Man

> my back
> is to the window
> I am
> in the public house
> sitting
> on foam and torn
> cloth
> glancing
> behind me from time
> to time
> into a void of churchy spires
> and soft
> blue
> I think
> I know
> the barman among the tobyjugs
> is dumbly
> mouthing the secret words
> IS
> HE
> BOTHERING
> YOU?
>
> it is
> slightly pouring down outside
> and inside I am shaking my
> head
> trying hard

not
to laugh
for
if I laugh or suggest
a smile
the man in the jacket
squelching beside me
who introduced himself to me nicely
will bash me with an iron bar
over
my head which will crunch
crack
in front of everyone
out
for a chat in familiar surroundings
safe
secure
just like he didn't do before
to somebody else he insists
He is
just out of Barlinnie
I am
glancing behind me from time
to
time
into a void of churchy blue
and soft
spires
I thought I
knew
so well So wrong

Goodnight John Boy

Action, adventure
and a long sea voyage that starts
at six in the morning
and all the Harlem whores

in hotel corridors
you can afford.   Someone young
and violent
turning the handle of your bedroom door
in the spooky dead of night
with only a chink of light
from the keyhole,
but don't be alarmed ladies and gentlemen

these chains are made of chrome steel
so unwrap the soap,
put your thumb in your mouth,
snuggle beneath Colonial sheets and think
of her cold shower junk-buck gymnastics.
The cockroach in the medicine cabinet,
the middle-aged negro with sweat
in his armpits in the yum yum sausage bar
looking for the syrup for the pancakes
'gimme some syrup, ah wawn some syrup'

of Abraham Lincoln
preaching peace but waging war
as he went marching through Georgia
pretending he was black
and wearing a top hat
and looking a bit like Jane Fonda's dad,
who is dead,
or Gregory Peck who isn't
but nothing at all like Buster Crabbe
who didn't know if he was Bucking
or Flashing or clean living Doris Day

with a cute button nose on the Deadwood stage
whip cracking away
if that's what

turns you on,
and King Kong climbing to the top
of the Empire State building
to have his wicked Simian way
a roll in the low budget hay with Fay Wray

in a torn silk dress
and strawberry blonde wig
or so we were led to believe
by the Senate of the day,
but I know for a fact he was a
regular, blueberry-pie guy
who beat up his wife between picking fights
with lame-brained lizards back on Skull Island
THE LAND OF OPPORTUNITY
where a puppet's gotta do
what a puppet's gotta do
and the niggers know their place
and that is trampled underfoot.
He only wanted to be loved

just like everybody else,
but he should have bought
a Statue of Liberty ashtray,
he should have bought a JFK rubber mask
to smother his conscience
just like everybody else
he should have heard the headboard
of the bed next door
slamming
against
the partition.
Ambulance music, steam hiss.
The smell of roasting chestnuts.
The smell of roasting gooks.   The smell
of Mary Tyler Moore

having her all-American breakdown.
And I should have known
that the bi-planes get us all in the end,
but I still stood up on the New York City subway
to give my seat to a woman
who looked at me as if I was a

Cream of Scottish Youth

rolled

trousers to knees and
danced a weird waltz.

Chucked bangers at club-feet,
snow at girls' faces,
crisp bags full of frogspawn slop.

Sat among rocks, wore Harlequin socks,
rabbit ear collars and baratheas, spat
on the heads of waggy yap dogs
allowed to run free by owners.
Rolled

jumper sleeves to elbows
and pretended to be Thalidomide.
Smoked
singles
bought from ice cream vans,
scuffed mushy leaves with best shoes, kicked
puddle-twigs at the dumb sun as the wind
swiped through big branches, scurried
among big shadows.
Tumbled,

yelling, from dizzy swish roundabouts,
pelted the swans in the dam with cans,
tore the pages from the brainyboy's books
then tipped his schoolbag upside down,
lit fires just for the hell of it, splashed
scruffy steam gold against the oaks

that had seen it all before.

Ate banana and marmite rolls
as gloom curdled in the cloakroom.
Looked at photos of whopper breasts,

studied photos of open legs,
fell over each other to sniff
the future.
Fumbled
in panties at puberty parties,
swallowed Pale Ale, Newcastle Brown,
Breaker Malt Liquor and Eldorado.
Gathered at night to sit on walls
or topple sun-dials onto grass.
Made scratchy marks on sheds and lamp-posts,
squirted stinking, chemist perfumes
onto clothes of teeth-brace boys,
spluttered over thick Panatellas,
chewed on borrowed plastic pipes.
Dropped lit matches into postboxes,
said the words 'fanny', 'gobble' and 'spunk',
spooned in shagalley toothpaste dark,
fell over each other to reach

the sex.
Grew
hair long, got it chopped off,
did everything wrong, everything
right.
Threw slushballs at respectable windows,
stones at clocks, rocks at stars
and cruised cobbled wynds with springs
in heels,
skated, laughing, into the void, fell over
each other to ask

the time.
Rolled

Trousers to knees and
danced a daft can-can.
Rolled back to ankles, hobbled
for home, the whipped

cream of Scotland's dream.

Ships

Me and Tommy, Warhol-lookalike,
lay in our bags on Sandy's floor
and watched him set fire to his pubic hair.

It was quite romantic, spectacular too.
Sandy framed in the big bay-window,
lights of Dumbarton twinkling behind him,
slow black shape of a passing ship.

A nasty smell and crackling sound.
We, nervously, laughed, Sandy the loudest.

He once wound a roll of sellotape
around a giggling, friendly girl,
and who was I to disagree
with the best artist I'd ever seen.

Sandy wasn't bothered though,
he scratched on his imitation 'Strad',
pissed through the hole of his favourite L.P.
I think
it was on the same night he lit up his hair.

'They were real goers,
the Knights of the Lower Floors'
he told me, often, and who was I . . .

Hadn't seen him for five years
until I saw him six years ago
drifting around in Glasgow Central.

We sat in a pub. I bought him a pint.
He doodled on soggy beermats.
He asked to sleep at mine that night,
I said we had visitors.
I'm sure he knew.

I haven't seen Tommy in ages either.

He had a birthmark on his leg.
He vomited out of a train window
on our way to visit Sandy.
I think it was
on the same night he pissed through the hole.

Daniel O'Rourke

Daniel O'Rourke

' I was born on July 5, 1959, in Port Glasgow. Back then, its reason was its river and its river was its reason. My father who had served his time in the Yards died a couple of years ago, no longer knowing what his home town was for. Mum was from County Antrim. It's romantic and sentimental, but I persist in thinking of myself as a Scot, in the original sense of the word, meaning Irish. Dad loved to sing and tell stories; my mother liked to reminisce – traits I hope my poetry has inherited.

As a poet unless (or until) you're very good, you are what you read. So Paul Blackburn's in there and Frank O'Hara and Tom Paulin and lots of the other mostly Irish and American writers I've lovingly ransacked since leaving Glasgow University in 1981. I don't think university taught me how to write poetry; but it probably taught me how to read it. I started writing in my early teens. Puberty, poetry and the guitar all seemed to arrive at around the same time and remain headily commingled in my memory. I wanted to be Leonard Cohen rather than Hugh MacDiarmid . . .

The discovery of a viably imagined Renfrewshire in the work of Alan Sharp, Bill Bryden, Peter McDougall, Gordon Williams and others made me want to try something other than song lyrics. Douglas Dunn had grown up in the next village; John Byrne had gone to my Paisley school. Poetry was not only permissible, it was possible.

But tricky. I was in my mid twenties before I happened upon anything resembling a voice of my own. Mind you, I took comfort from the fact that so many Scottish poets didn't hit their stride until they were older than any of the writers in this anthology: Muir, MacCaig, Morgan, late developers, every one.

Poems come or they don't; I can't command them. Being prone to hero worship, and making my living from arts television, I fill too many of those that do come with other people's art instead of my own life. And I still spend more time reading great poems by other poets than trying to write good ones of my own. Although I've done my share of teaching and thoroughly enjoy it, it's time poetry took its degree and left university. Well, I would say that, aiming as I do to write poems as immediate and accessible as the folk and pop songs that got me started in the first place.

Frank O'Hara reckoned only three American poets were better than going to the movies. To find out which three, read O'Hara – you should anyway. That's the challenge. Poems have to be good enough to compete not just with other poems, but to take their chances out there in a crowded, cozening, culture. I'd like my poems to have as much appeal as my programmes. Let's hope the best is yet to come. **'**

Publications:

Second Cities (Vennel Press, 1991)

Gold

Through a wine glass today in a Soho bistro
I saw you dear ghost of 1979.
Micro skirt and air wear shoes, those red
Framed specs that telly people pick
To filter histories out. You were with a louche
And deferential, slightly younger man.
Watching you trump his Amex Gold
With your own glistering plastic
I thought of nights in the city of Glasgow
When all the gold you wanted
Was the light of my open door.

Robbie

We shouldered you out into a cold blue morning,
the pig iron kind all keepers hate

when limbs get skinned and balls bounce high.
There was a cross wind blowing from the Firth –

a day for inswingers; though corners
never troubled you who'd have got both hands

on the moon, given a two yard run at it.
No, your weakness was the fierce first timer

cleverly kept down, the only way we ever
got you out, playing 'Three and In',

on your well kept Gourock lawn,
replaying the war years

when you were Cappielow's number one,
saving penalties like ration coupons.

To The Telegraph then, Robbie,
you were Morton's Miracle Man Between The Sticks,

invincible in polo neck and bunnet –
old goalie a league of ailments

couldn't beat, till a cunning cancer
aimed one low.

Crystal

I had forgotten how tiny the glasses were;
a house of sticky Christmas drinks.
Glugging whisky into mugs I see you grue
at Tio Pepe presented in error
so many long first foots ago
before we learned of drams or death –
cups too bitter for liqueur glasses:
that crystal is all I'll take
from this house we've come to close.

Algren

I picture you profiled in Film Noir tones
shirt-sleeves rolled back, cigar smoke

coiling like an unpent spring
as you type at a card table

in some Clark St. cathouse
in '48 or '49

before Korea and McCarthy
made it hard for Reds to work.

The book you're writing,
'The Man with the Golden Arm'

will make a movie star of Sinatra
and not one royalty cent for you

last of the bare-knuckle poets,
more famous in the end

for being the first man
to make Simone de Beauvoir come

than for anything you wrote.
Travelling to Chicago

and later, here in the burg
you called a busted flush,

I read 'The Neon Wilderness'
and 'City on the Make'

serenades to the low lives
and losers of these streets.

As well, after your hobo
wanderings, the time you did

for stealing a typewriter,
that you remained constant to Chicago

her soda jerks and crap games
pastures new then

reduced to scuffed
green baize.

Great Western Road

Glasgow, you look beatific in blue
and I've a Saturday before me
for galleries and poems,
a house full of Haydn,
and beneath my kitchen window,
tennis stars in saris
lobbing backhands at the bins.
French coffee, and who knows maybe
Allen Ginsberg in my bath!
then round to the dairy
where scones are cooling on the rack
and Jimmy won't let me leave
till I've tried one there and then,
here, where the new Glasgow started –
an old grey city going blonde
whose Asian shops are full of fruits
we owe to Cap'n Bligh
and I'm so juiced I could walk clear
to Loch Lomond,
past busses stripping the willow
all along Great Western Road
but I just browse bargains in banjos
and pop-art knitted ties,
before checking out the crime section
at Caledonian Books,
finding Friesias in the flowershops
and in the second hand record store,
Bruckner's Third,
The Cleveland
under Szell:
so sad; like falling for passing students
with that black haired, blue eyed look,
or buying basil and chorizos . . .
In the afternoon I'll look at paintings
in Dougie Thomson's Mayfest show,
maybe stroll down to the studio
to view some archive film,
past the motorways and multi-storeys

of Grieve's Ultimate Cowcaddens,
the peeling pawn at George's Cross
where, today, everything is redeemable
because tonight there'll be guitar poets
from Russia at the Third Eye Centre.
And later I'll cook zarzuela
for a new and nimble friend.
God Glasgow it's glorious
just to gulp you down in heartfuls,
feeling something quite like love.

L. Himid

Maud Sulter

❛ I was born in the Southern General Hospital in Glasgow at 1am on the morning of the 19th of September under the zodiac sign of Virgo in the Chinese year of the Rat.

As a child I attended Wolsely Street Primary School in Oatlands and as a young adult Adelphi Secondary School in the Gorbals. The primary school was demolished in the early 1970s and the secondary school is no longer functioning as such. In my writing I often address issues of lost and disputed territories, both psychological and physical.

The poem 'As a Blackwoman' was written in London in 1984. It is a polemic about the historical invasion of the Black female body and the necessity for all women to have control over their own bodies in a world where, in the U.S. alone, 52% of women with AIDS are black; black people live 6 years less than white folk, and Blackwomen stand a 1 in 104 chance of being murdered compared to 1 in 369 for white women.

The title, *As A Blackwoman*, was chosen by Desmond Johnson, the editor and publisher of my first collection of poetry which was published by Akira Press in 1985. It was one of their initial publications of books by poets and authors of the African diaspora.

The central body of my poetic works is unequivocally the love poetry which is addressed to both genders. 'Passion Plays', 'Drich Day' and 'If Leaving You' are taken from a cycle of poems published in *As A Blackwoman* (1985).

The cycle deals with a brief love affair between myself and Larry Waldren, an African American male, whom I met at the Edinburgh Festival in the Fall of 1984 while he was working as an administrator of The Negro Ensemble Company. The New York based Company, which was founded by Doug Turner Ward, was on tour with *A Soldier's Play* by Charles Fuller.

Larry and I later spent time together in New York in an apartment on Bleeker Street in Greenwich Village which he rented. It was my first visit to the U.S. The love affair cooled during the trip but my passion for New York continues unabated. ❜

As a Blackwoman

As a blackwoman
the bearing of my child
is a political act.

I have
been mounted in rape
    bred from like cattle
    mined for my fecundity

I have
been denied abortion
    denied contraception
    denied my freedom to choose

I have
been subjected to abortion
    injected with contraception
    sterilised without my consent

I have
borne witness to the murders
of my children
by the Klan, the Front, the State

I have
borne sons hung for rape
for looking at a white girl

I have
borne daughters shot
for being liberationists

As a blackwoman
I have taken the power to choose
to bear a black child
– a political act?

As a blackwoman

every act is a personal act
every act is a political act

As a blackwoman
the personal is political
holds no empty rhetoric.

Passion Plays

Passion plays on the lips
like guilt preys on the mind.

Having left you
not five minutes ago
I try to remember

Your eyes – piercing
your broad smile and your
built for speed hips

Fearful that not having you near me
my memory will deceive me.

That the opportunity was there
to touch you
caress you
to kiss those bold black lips

Yet denied myself the pleasure
Erzulie hear me sister

The train bullets through
a dark dank tunnel
close my eyes   purse my lips
heart pumping fast   in anticipation

Of your mouth moist touching mine
the charge between us

makes me start back
in to my corner seat.

Tomorrow my candy   my caramel sweet
we two in Edinburgh shall meet

Drich Day

Ice cold steel gray sky ahead
entering the Kingdom of Fife

Walk through ruins
of castles ancient, a priory
tombstones cold as death itself
of people past, children lost
to disease poverty the harsh
reality of life

Sea a blanket of September sorrows
unremitting drich and drizzle
permeates our light outerwear

Walking the links at St Andrews
we kissed holding each to the other
treasuring the moment
for the sake of itself
nothing between us and Denmark
except that tomorrow you leave me.

If Leaving You

If leaving you
was as easy
as the falling

in love
with
a
total
stranger

– not total

our blackness
a bond
before speech
or encounter

I could walk
from you now
into the hustle
and bustle
of Waverley
station
and checking
my ticket
– depart.

Jackie Kay

Jackie Kay

❛ I was born in 1961 and brought up in Scotland. *The Adoption Papers* (Bloodaxe, 1991) won an Eric Gregory award, a Scottish Arts Council Award, a Forward Poetry award, and a Saltire award. It was originally broadcast on Radio 3 as part of the *Drama Now* series.

My first play *Chiaroscuro* was first presented by Theatre of Black Women in 1986 and is published by Methuen in *Lesbian Plays*. My second, *Twice Over*, was presented by Gay Sweatshop in 1988 and is published by Methuen in *Gay Sweatshop: Four Plays and a Company*. It has had productions in Vancouver and San Francisco.

My television work includes *Hidden Fears*, a short drama for school children about AIDS, and *Twice Through the Heart*, a poetry documentary for BBC 2 about a woman who murdered her husband.

Two's Company (Blackie, 1992) is my first collection of poetry for children. *Every Bit of It*, a play about Bessie Smith, was presented by the Sphinx Theatre Company in 1992–93.

Twilight Shift, a play about two male lovers in the mining community, will be presented by 7:84 Theatre Company this coming autumn.

My second collection of poetry for adults, *Other Lovers*, will be published by Bloodaxe this September. ❜

Chapter 3: The Waiting Lists

The first agency we went to
didn't want us on their lists,
we didn't live close enough to a church
nor were we church-goers
(though we kept quiet about being communists).
The second told us
we weren't high enough earners.
The third liked us
but they had a five-year waiting list.
I spent six months trying not to look
at swings nor the front of supermarket trolleys,
not to think this kid I've wanted could be five.
The fourth agency was full up.
The fifth said yes but again no babies.
Just as we were going out the door
I said oh you know we don't mind the colour.
Just like that, the waiting was over.

This morning a slim manilla envelope arrives
postmarked Edinburgh: one piece of paper
I have now been able to look up your microfiche
(as this is all the records kept nowadays).
From your mother's letters, the following information:
Your mother was nineteen when she had you.
You weighed eight pounds four ounces.
She liked hockey. She worked in Aberdeen
as a waitress. She was five foot eight inches.

I thought I'd hid everything
that there wasnie wan
giveaway sign left

I put Marx Engels Lenin (no Trotsky)
in the airing cupboard – she'll no be
checking out the towels surely

All the copies of the *Daily Worker*
I shoved under the sofa

the dove of peace I took down from the loo

A poster of Paul Robeson
saying give him his passport
I took down from the kitchen

I left a bust of Burns
my detective stories
and the Complete Works of Shelley

She comes at 11.30 exactly.
I pour her coffee
from my new Hungarian set

And foolishly pray she willnae
ask its origins – honestly
this baby is going to my head.

She crosses her legs on the sofa
I fancy I hear the *Daily Workers*
rustle underneath her

Well she says, you have an interesting home
She sees my eyebrows rise.
It's different she qualifies.

Hell and I've spent all morning
trying to look ordinary
– a lovely home for the baby.

She buttons her coat all smiles
I'm thinking
I'm on the home run

But just as we get to the last post
her eye catches at the same times as mine
a red ribbon with twenty world peace badges

Clear as a hammer and sickle
on the wall.
Oh, she says are you against nuclear weapons?

To Hell with this. Baby or no baby.
Yes I says. Yes yes yes.
I'd like this baby to live in a nuclear free world.

Oh. Her eyes light up.
I'm all for peace myself she says,
and sits down for another cup of coffee.

Chapter 6: The Telling Part

Ma mammy bot me oot a shop
Ma mammy says I was a luvly baby

Ma mammy picked me (I wiz the best)
your mammy had to take you (she'd no choice)

Ma mammy says she's no really ma mammy
(just kid on)

It's a bit like a part you've rehearsed so well
you can't play it on the opening night
She says my real mammy is away far away
Mammy why aren't you and me the same colour
But I love my mammy whether she's real or no
My heart started rat tat tat like a tin drum
all the words took off to another planet
Why

But I love ma mammy whether she's real or no

I could hear the upset in her voice
I says *I'm not your real mother,*
though Christ knows why I said that,
If I'm not who is, but all my planned speech
went out the window

She took me when I'd nowhere to go
my mammy is the best mammy in the world OK.

After mammy telt me she wisnae my real mammy
I was scared to death she was gonnie melt
or something or mibbe disappear in the dead
of night and somebody would say she wis a fairy
godmother. So the next morning I felt her skin
to check it was flesh, but mibbe it was just
a good imitation. How could I tell if my mammy
was a dummy with a voice spoken by someone else?
So I searches the whole house for clues
but I never found nothing. Anyhow a day after
I got my guinea pig and forgot all about it.

I always believed in the telling anyhow.
You can't keep something like that secret
I wanted her to think of her other mother
out there, thinking that child I had will be
seven today eight today all the way up to
god knows when. I told my daughter –
I bet your mother's never missed your birthday,
how could she?

Mammy's face is cherries.
She is stirring the big pot of mutton soup
singing *I gave my love a cherry*
it had no stone.
I am up to her apron.
I jump onto her feet and grab her legs
like a huge pair of trousers,
she walks round the kitchen lifting me up.

Suddenly I fall off her feet.
And mammy falls to the floor.
She won't stop the song
I gave my love a chicken it had no bone.
I run next door for help.
When me and Uncle Alec come back
Mammy's skin is toffee stuck to the floor.
And her bones are all scattered like toys.

Now when people say 'ah but
it's not like having your own child though is it',

I say of course it is, what else is it?
she's my child, I have told her stories
wept at her losses, laughed at her pleasures,
she is mine.

I was always the first to hear her in the night
all this umbilical knot business is nonsense
– the men can afford deeper sleeps that's all.
I listened to hear her talk,
and when she did I heard my voice under hers
and now some of her mannerisms crack me up

Me and my best pal
don't have Donny Osmond or David Cassidy
on our walls and we don't wear Starsky and Hutch
jumpers either. Round at her house we put on
the old record player and mime to Pearl Bailey
Tired of the life I lead, tired of the blues I breed
and Bessie Smith I can't do without my kitchen man.
Then we practise ballroom dancing giggling,
everyone thinks we're dead old-fashioned.

Close Shave

The only time I forget is down the pit
right down in the belly of it,
my lamp shining like a third eye,
my breath short and fast like my wife's
when she's knitting. Snip snap.
I've tried to tell her as many times
as I've been down this mine. I can't
bring myself to, she'd tell our girls
most probably. It doesn't bear thinking.

Last night he shaved me again.
Close. Such an act of trust.
And he cut my hair; the scissors snip
snipped all night as I lay beside Ella

(Good job she's not that interested)
I like watching him sweep it up.
He holds the brush like a dancing partner,
short steps, fox trot: 4/4 time.
I knew from the first time, he did too

Our eyes met when he came
to the bit above my lip. 6 years ago.
We've only slept the night together twice:
once when my wife's sister died,
once when the brother-in-law committed suicide.
She left our daughters behind that time.
My nerves made me come too quick
but I liked sleeping in his smooth arms
till dawn. He was gone

Before they woke, giggling round breakfast.
He says nobody else can cut my curls.
I laughed loud for the first time since
God knows when. You're too vain man.
We kissed, I like his beard on my skin,
how can you be a barber with a beard
I said to him; it's my daughters that worry me.
Course I can never tell the boys down the pit.
When I'm down here I work fast so it hurts.

Lighthouse Wall

(for Derek Hughes)

Somewhere beyond the thin lighthouse wall
I can feel him pulling me; hard tug of a net.
I can see his face, laughing and wet rising
out of the waves, the cold Atlantic sea,
that holiday. That was some holiday: sex maybe
three, four times a day. He's urging me on – why
wait, why bother hanging on

My body is cold. I call my nurse all the time.
I have a thing that I squeeze and it bleeps him.
He has a nice little bottom. I'd love to pinch it.
In the hours when I am lucid I am so aware
of my body shrinking. I imagine I might just disappear
into the white cotton. I hold onto the hands of friends.
They start to merge together

In the hours – what kind of hours would you call
these? More like years, epochs, centuries one day
and a split second blink if you miss it another day.
I try and follow the clock on the wall. The little hand.
The big hand. It's all pointless. I take my glasses off.
I put my glasses on. On and off on and off off and
the hands still the same time.

Today I'm having a blood transfusion. I am cold.
I ask the nurse for another blanket. He tells me
I am warm. I don't argue anymore. I haven't got
what? strength or time. I hate this though – self-pity:
I wrap it round myself like a velvet cloak or mist
from the sea; which sea would that be? The Black Sea.
The Red Sea. The North Sea.

I am running somewhere by the Baltic Sea; my body
is strong and fit. There is a space I can fall into.
There he is. His floral trunks. His forest legs.
It is quiet. I am full of awe. I kiss the salt
from his shoulders. He is rock hard. The long long
stretch of white sand is empty. The wind whips.
At last, I know this hand.

Pounding Rain

News of us spreads like a storm.
The top of our town to the bottom.
We stand behind curtains
parted like hoods; watch each other's eyes.

We talk of moving to the west end,
this bit has always been a shoe box
tied with string; but then again
your father still lives in that house
where we warmed up spaghetti bolognese
in lunch hours and danced to Louis Armstrong,
his gramophone loud as our two heart beats
going boom diddy boom diddy boom.

Did you know then? I started dating Davy;
when I bumped into you I'd just say Hi.
I tucked his photo booth smile into my satchel
brought him out for my pals in the intervals.

A while later I heard you married Trevor Campbell.
Each night I walked into the school dinner hall
stark naked, till I woke to Miss, Miss Miss
every minute. Then, I bumped into you at the Cross.

You haven't changed you said; that reassurance.
Nor you; your laugh still crosses the street.
I trace you back, beaming, till –
Why don't you come round, Trevor would love it.

He wasn't in. I don't know how it happened.
We didn't bother with a string of do you remembers.
I ran my fingers through the beads in your hair.
Your hair's nice I said stupidly, nice, suits you.

We sat and stared till our eyes filled
like a glass of wine. I did it, the thing
I'd dreamt a million times. I undressed you
slowly, each item of clothing fell
with a sigh. I stroked your silk skin
until we were back in the Campsies, running
down the hills in the pounding rain,
screaming and laughing; soaked right through.

W. N. Herbert

❛ I was born in 1961 in Dundee, where I grew up in a succession of archetypal dwellings: the tenement, the multi-storey, the bungalow. When I was eighteen I went to Brasenose College, Oxford from a misbegotten desire to master English literature at its cultural heart. I got a first, and began a doctorate on Hugh MacDiarmid – a first for Oxford. Around this time I began to use Scots, not out of duty, but because the poetry I was writing wouldn't work until I reproduced the gull-like tones of my origins. In 1989, with Richard Price, I launched the magazine *Gairfish*. After the publication of my thesis as *To Circumjack MacDiarmid*, I held a Writer's Residency in Dumfries and Galloway. In October 1993 I took up a second residency in Morayshire.

My experience of being Scottish in England was the discovery of suppressed contrasts. Unlike Ireland, Scotland is not supposed to be 'different' or 'foreign'. It is the country which is not quite a country, possessing a language which is not really a language. To use only English or Scots, then, seems to cover up some aspect of our experience, to 'lie'. The truth about Scotland, perhaps, can only be situated between the dominant and suppressed parts of language, in the region of the forked tongue.

So I write in both English and Scots. In each of these I could be accused of lying. In Scots I pretend that my basic speech – Dundonian – hasn't been atrophied by cultural neglect, and still has access to the broad vocabulary of the Scots dictionary. This creates the language of a quasi-fictional country, one which offers a critique of the present status of 'Scotland'.

In English I don't lie so much as hope: that an English audience is engaged by the depiction of an challengingly 'other' culture; and that my Scottish audience has a mind of its own. *The Cortina Sonata*, the sequence from which these English poems come, imitates the form of the classical sonata to present its cultural and autobiographical themes as complex, lively, and, hopefully, harmonious. ❜

Publications:

Sterts and Stobies (with Robert Crawford) (Obog Books, 1985)
Severe Burns (with Robert Crawford and David Kinloch) (Obog Books, 1987)

Other Tongues (with Meg Bateman, David Kinloch and Angela McSeveney) (Verse, 1990)
Sharawaggi (with Robert Crawford) (Polygon, 1990)
The Landfish, (Duncan of Jordanstone, 1991)
Dundee Doldrums (Galliard, 1991)
Anither Music, (Vennel, 1991)
The Testament of the Reverend Thomas Dick (Littlewood Arc, 1993)

forthcoming

Forked Tongue (Bloodaxe, 1994)

Mappamundi

Eh've wurkt oot a poetic map o thi warld.

Vass tracts o land ur penntit reid tae shaw
Englan kens naethin aboot um. Ireland's
bin shuftit tae London, whaur
oafficis o thi Poetry Sock occupeh fehv
squerr mile. Seamus Heaney occupehs three
o thon. Th'anerly ithir bits in Britain
ur Oaxfurd an Hull. Thi Pool, Scoatlan,
an Bisley, Stroud, ur cut ti cuttilbanes in
America, which issa grecht big burdcage wi
a tartan rug owre ut, tae shaw
Roabirt Lowell. Chile disnae exist.
Argentina's bin beat. Hungary and Russia
haena visas. Africa's editid doon ti
a column in *Poetry Verruca*,
whaur Okigbo's gote thi ghaist
o Roy Campbill hingin owre um. Thi Faur East's
faan aff – aa but China: thon's renemmed
Ezra Poond an pit in thi croncit cage.
France disnae get a luke-in:
accoardin tae Geoffrey Hill, plucky wee
Charles Péguy is wrasslin wi
this big deid parrot caad "Surrealism" fur
thi throne o Abstinthe Sorbet.

In this scenario Eh'm a bittern stoarm aff Ulm.

2nd Doldrum (Elephants Graveyard)

Whaur ur yi Dundee? Whaur's yir Golem buriit?
Whaur doon yir pendies lurks it?
Broon brick, eldscoorit, timedustchoakit,
blin windies – whaur's MaGonnagal's hert?
Creh o seagulls echoes thru closies' lugs:

nithin but 'iz hertsherds, shatterit, deidtrootdreh,
nithin but vishuns o lehburers deean.

Eh kent yi i thi street; Peddie Street,
whaur boarn an raisd in tenements
ma sowelclert sheppit; Eh spoattit yi
certin a wheelbarra ower cobblies
(ower tarmaccadum and undir um's thi cobblestanes,
deid buriit jaabanes o yir weans' hopes),
Eh saw yiz in grey overalls, een deid an blank,
heid bulletgrey an taursmearit, durt
clung til yir een,
and indivisibul fae yir past,
oot o thi fremms o photygraphs
waulkin weldit tae wheelbarra,
haunds soldert tae toil, an nae rest.

Ghaist o thi Thurties, Dundee whan thi Daith cam doon,
grey sinders descendin, meldit wi claiths an dreams,
Dundee whan Amerika fell,
Dundee whan thi Depreshun cam owerseas
an bidit, an restit in oor faithirs' braces –
oor flatbunnits! oor bandylegs! oor rickets!
Waulkin uppa street, a deid, a ghostie,
a passedby, a damnit, a wurkir –
ghaist restless and nivir kennin green.

Pendies – lanes; closies – tenement entrances; sowelclert – soulclay;
weans – children; bidit – stayed, remained.

A Backlook

(To my father)

Presleyan, yi didnae waant
ti be a tigir

rinnan aflemm thru gloaman
o tennyments
hittan thir tap-note o grey,
Sportan Post tichtfurlit in
yir haund.
Uncranglan lyk
a quiff, i thi glistiry room
whaur men ur biddubil.

Gloaman – early evening; uncranglan – uncurling, relaxing; glistiry – hot, sweaty, flickering with light; biddubil – cowed, obedient.

The Renaissance of Song

Yince auld mithir Lirklips
hoolocht owre thi land
inna cauld sea's grouse an grue,
an doon thi sealblack deeps,
thi weelthrainit steps;

nae camera cud recaa
hoo dumbfounert aa'ur weans
did stare aboot lyk hotties, then,
did thirsty raise
a renaissance o sang!

Hoolocht – rolled like a rockslide; land – a floor of a tenement, both the level and the area between doors and stairs; grue – shiver with fear, cold or repulsion; weelthrainit – worn by constant use, like a familiar tune; hotties – those who have some message pinned to their backs of which they are unaware.

The Gairfish

'At first sight, it would be thought beneficial to the salmon fishing,
if a method could be invented, by which the porpoises, or Gairfish as
they are called, which devour so many salmon, might be destroyed.'
        P. Monifieth, Forfars. Statist. Acc., xiii. 493

Lyk a selkie orran ottir wad yi be,
takin a glammach frae thae fozie saumon
            that wad cam back tae Scoatlan?
Ach porpy, bricht sea-pollock, yi sud ken
thi bourgeois winnae staun fur that;
            selkith can he see ablow
thi seaweed, seeminsolid, risin inna promontory
that tae thi tide's tug shufts: here thi gairfush gaes –
shooin thi waatir's brim in carefu slytes
            that laive aa boats ahent:
yir thochtliss scrift.
            Selkith can thi bourgeois hear
yir screnoch seep atween thi crancrums
o thi drivin seas –
                        Aa he kens is sum buggir's et
            his saumonses, and's tint thi'orts.

            'But' (he sez), 'thi gairfush nivir biggit aucht,
nivir scrievd a sang.'
(Nor did thi Homeridai till
Peisistratos saw thi gree!)
            'Thi gairfush nivir foond th'ile.'
(Or nivir let oan, gin they did!) –
            Thi gairfush pollutit nary an ocean,
            thi gairfush nivir inventit thi Boamb,
thi gairfush nivir profitit fae onywan's lehbur,
'Therefore,
            therefore . . .'

But aye til them that tak thi doondrag oan;
them that dallow i thi doggerlone o Poetese,
            plootir amang sejoinit wurds,

       yi gleesh ayont th'offskep,
sloom ablow thi mairchent's gaff –
Aye yi seem tae them thon gairfush Arion rade,
baith ploongan and ascendan
i thi dance o sunlicht aff yir freithy plumashe –
       An thi splores fae'iz despirate mooth,
       singan fur dear life!

Gee th'ogertfou yir Giaconda's smickir;
gink at thi Courier's unca-richt rant;
doistir oot thi Bummir's caas
    wi whut we'd cry a Socialist sang:
       'Here i thi sea
       wi tak as wi need
       an gee whitsoivir
       wi hae ti gee.'
  – That'll shak'um i thir baffies! That'll
threip thir panloaf mugs
intil thir tabnabs!

O meenistirs & meenistirs' wives, auld leddies ivry-
                        whaur,
Jutelairds' ghaists & thi faceliss face
   that 'rins' wir deean facktries
                  – Here's a force
that nivir dossis, swimman in thir sleep;
a dab haund at cullin prickirs tae, whit's mair.
Here's a waukindreme tae mak yi girle:

    a skail o gairfush, omnegaddrums,
    wi a thoosan makars oan thir backs,
    snoovin up thi Tay thiday,
    sall raise a sang lyk smirr tae faa
    upo thi wurkirs' polly-shees
    an gar thum hyne yiz aa awa!
    Thir plisky spit sall gar yi think
    thi daith-dive's rinnin frae yir lugs
    an dreepan frae yir toaffy nebs!

    An this sall be a smorethow
    upo yir bourgeois pow:
    luke up: ut's faain NOW!

Gairfush – porpoise (the word is peculiar to the vicinity of Dundee); *selkie* – seal (believed by the Gaelic peoples to be capable of human form); *glammach* – a snapped-up morsel; *fozie* – dullwitted; *porpy, sea pollock* – names for the porpoise; *selkith* – seldom; *shooin* – sewing; *slytes* – smooth sharp movements; *scrifts* – fluent improvisations; *screnoch* – shrill cry; *crancrums* – things difficult to understand (here, fig., the currents); *tint* – lost, left; *orts* – what is left of food after the best has been extracted; *biggit* – built; *scrievd* – wrote; *doondrag* – the incumbent weight of a sin or disgrace to a family; *doggerlone* – wreck; *plootir* – splash heavily; *sejoinit* – disjuncted; *gleesh* – burn with a hard, steady flame; *offskep* – the utmost boundary of a landscape (here, the sea); *sloom* – move slowly and silently; *plumashe* – plume of feathers (here, fig., foam); *splores* – drops of saliva ejected whilst speaking (or singing); *ogertfou* – drunk with a sense of one's own good taste; *smickir* – grin; *gink* – titter to oneself; *unca-richt* – self-satisfied, hypocritical; *doistir* – thunder; *Bummirs* – factory hooters; *baffies* – slippers; *panloaf* – affected, snobbish; *tabnabs* – tea-things; *Jutelairds* – those who, in the latter part of the last century and the first part of this, made their fortunes from Dundee's jute mills; *dosses* – snoozes, is lazy; *prickirs* – basking sharks, tailors; *girle* – having the teeth set on edge; *skail* – both a school and a storm; *omnegaddrums* – a miscellaneous collection, a medley, the unincorporated craftsmen of the burgh; *snoovin* – sliding easily; *smirr* – fine rain; *polly-shee* – a pulley attached to a pole, from which a rope runs to a window, for hanging clothes to dry (another word peculiar to Dundee); *gar* – make; *hyne* – hoist; *plisky* – tricky; *daith-dive* – putrid moisture from the body's orifices after death; *smorethow* – heavy fall of snow that threatens to smother; *pow* – forehead.

Coco-De-Mer

Dinna bathir wi thi braiggil o wir lends
that maks a cothaman o gravy
i thi cot, but famine in wir crullit herts –
let gae oan thi dumbswaul, be
brankie i thi breakirs, an flocht,

flocht lyk thi crospunk intae Lewis –
thi lucky-bean tae thi haunds o thi misk.

*Braiggil – an old and dangerously rickety article; lends – loins;
cothaman – surfeit; crullit – cowering; dumbswaul – a long, noiseless
sea-swell in calm, windless weather; brankie – pranked-up; crospunk
– the Molucca bean, drifted to the shores of some of the Western
Islands; misk – land covered in coarse, moorish grasses.*

Mariposa Pibroch

If the Grunewald *Crucifixions's* like
the skeleton of a butterfly, that

gnarling into the blackish, ragged
filaments through which my memory

is falling into the back garden
like pancake-large snowflakes;

then the mosquito I pressed against
this kitchen window yesterday,

the emptiness between its sap and
the pulse of my apologising finger,

is bringing me back, like swinging
from a balcony by the nail caught

in my jean's rump; landing in Elie,
in the grounds of a manse, cruciform,

clouting the earth like a sack
of floury potatoes, back emptied

of air. I'm facing a piper outside
Selfridges, playing airs sentimental

enough to summon drunks to shake
my penniless hands and beg; airs

that are built into the childhood
but aren't genuine. The giant

mosquito drone that alone demarks this
foreign music I feel kin to, salutes

or seems to the offerings I cannot
make: only the hearing is authentic.

Dingle Dell

There is no passport to this country,
it exists as a quality of the language.

It has no landscape you can visit;
when I try to listen to its vistas

I don't think of that round tower, though
only two exist in Scotland, though

both are near me. There are figures on
an aunt's old clock, cottars; Scots

as marketed to Scots in the last century:
these are too late. I seek something

between troughs, a green word dancing
like weed in a wave's translucence,

a pane not smashed for an instance
through which the Dingle Dell of Brechin

sinks into the park like a giant's grave
from which his bones have long since

walked on air. Into this hole in
the gums of the language I see a name

roll like a corpse into the plague pits:
Bella. It is both my grandmothers'.

Beauty, resilient as girstle, reveals
itself: I see all of Scotland

rolling down and up on death's yoyo.
There is no passport to this country.

Kathleen Jamie

❝ What can I say? I'm thirty-one, and have been writing for half of my life. Now I'm staring at this piece of paper trying to tell something about that writing and that life, without sounding portentous. For the ~~fifth~~ sixth time I tear it up and start again.

I got into university, with difficulty, and studied philosophy. Before that, there was my family, home and school – I remember kicking very hard against the small options which seemed to be our lot, as though I'd glimpsed a huge world but felt it was being withheld from me. Nowadays I feel part of it. Maybe my poems are the place where I make exchanges with the world.

There are figures in much of my work; queens, princesses, anchorites, wandering monks. I think these are forms of energy; or aspects of the self, like the figures on tarot cards. I think my work is a means of exploration for me. Some explorations result in dead-ends.

I can't answer the question 'why do you write?' In bursts of enthusiasm I have tried to be a 'woman writer' and a 'Scottish writer' but grow irritated and feel confined. I have no motives, certainly no 'message', but I would like to write some very good poems. ❞

Publications:

Black Spiders (Salamander Press, 1982)
A Flame in Your Heart with Andrew Greig (Bloodaxe, 1986)
The Way We Live (Bloodaxe, 1987)
The Golden Peak (Virago, 1992)
The Autonomous Region (with photographs by Sean Mayne Smith) (Bloodaxe, 1993)

Forthcoming:

The Queen of Sheba (Bloodaxe, 1994)

The Republic of Fife

Higher than the craw-stepped
gables of our institutes – chess-clubs,
fanciers, reels & Strathspeys –
the old kingdom of lum, with crowns agley.

All birds will be citizens: banners
of starlings; Jacobin crows – also:
Sonny Jim Aitken, Special P.C.
whose red face closed in polis cars

utters *terrible, ridiculous*
at his brother and sister citizens
but we're no feart, not of anyone
with a tartan nameplate screwed to his door.

Citizen also: the tall fellow I watched
lash his yurt to the leafy earth,
who lifted his chin
to my greeting, roared AYE!

as in YES! FOREVER! MYSELF!
The very woods where my friend Isabel
once saw a fairy, blue as a gas flame
dancing on trees. All this

close to the motorway
where a citizen has dangled,
maybe with a friend clutching
his/her ankles to spray

PAY NO POLL TAX on a flyover
near to Abernethy, in whose tea rooms
old Scots kings and bishops in mitres
supped wi a lang spoon. Citizens:

our spires and doocoots
institutes and tinkies' benders,
old Scots kings and dancing fairies

give strength to my house

on whose roof we can balance,
carefully stand and see
clear to the far off mountains,
cities, rigs and gardens,

Europe, Africa, the Forth and Tay bridges,
even dare let go, lift our hands
and wave to the waving citizens
of all those other countries.

A Shoe

On the dry sand of Cramond I found
            a huge
                    platform sole, a wedge
of rubber gateau among the o-so
rounded pebbles
                    the occasional
washed up san-pro.

I could arrange it in the bathroom
with the pretty
                    Queeny shells, God,
we'd laugh, wouldn't we, girls?

                    Those bloody bells
ringing down corridors
hauling us this way and that;
    wee sisters and pals
        tugging our hair,
            folders, books
and those shoes–stupid
as a moon walker's; ah,
            the comfort of gravity.

You don't suppose she just
                    stepped off the Forth Bridge,

head over heels, shoes self-righting,
          like a cat,
hair and arms flying up
    as she slid down through the water?

Or did she walk in, saying yes
         I recognise this
as the water yanked heavy
    on thighs belly breasts?

God, girls, we'd laugh: –
         it's alright once you're in.
it's alright
         once you're out the other side.

Hand Relief

Whatever happened to friends like Liz,
who curled her legs on a leather settee,
and touched your knee, girl/girl,
as she whispered what the businessmen of Edinburgh
wear beneath their suits –

laughed and hooked her hair back
saying Tuesday, giving some bloke
hand relief, she'd looked up at the ceiling
for the hundredth time that lunch-hour,
and screaming, slammed the other hand down hard
on the panic button; had to stand there
topless in front of the bouncers
and the furious punter, saying
sorry, I'm sorry, it was just a spider. .

Whatever happens to girls like Liz
fresh out of school, at noon on a Saturday
waiting for her shift at Hotspots
sauna, in a dressing gown
with a pink printed bunny

who follows you to the window
as you look out at the city
and calls you her pal. She says, *you're a real pal.*

Things which never shall be

I shall be your wife.
Behind the doors of our house
which are wooden, and plentiful:
dogs and other animals, eager to play.
Rooms of grasses and flowers give out
to further rooms, our house
will be settled among woodland and hills.
So go. And take the dogs with you.
Leave me to work and fecundity in everything:
trees, hedgerows, weather-signs, poetry,
quirks you'll love and mock
only in jest. Our bedroom
will gather bouquets of sunshine,
we'll be home there in winter, I'll play
the spirit and you'll catch your breath.
We'll inhabit a huge place,
where I could move between rooms
with books in my arms,
and our home will be home to all comers.
We'll become skilled in art and endurance,
experts in love, and each other.

Ships/rooms

Though I love this travelling life and yearn
like ships docked, I long
for rooms to open with my bare hands,
and there discover the wonderful, say

a ship's prow rearing, and a ladder
of rope thrown down.
Though young, I'm weary:
I'm all rooms at present, all doors
fastened against me;
but once admitted I crave
and swell for a fine, listing ocean-going prow
no man in creation can build me.

Permanent cabaret

Our highwire artiste,
knowing nothing of fear, will take
sparkling risks fifty feet high.
Her costume, ladies, is iced with
hard diamonds.
While she mounts all those steps
our old friend the clown will stand
upside down in a shower of confetti
and chirp 'Love me!'

Their lamp is the last on camp to go out.
Coco reads Jung, sometimes aloud to
Estelle, if she's sewing on sequins.
More often she practises alone in the ring
for the day she enters permanent cabaret,
perhaps in Zurich. Coco cracks his knuckles,
thinking vaguely of children, or considers
repainting the outside of their van.

Half way across Estelle glitters like frost.
She has frozen. 'Remain professional.' She
draws breath through her teeth, wavers
her hand: 'Let Coco sense something for once!'
His red boots are edging towards her. He
coaxes, offers aid – his absurd umbrella.
The audience wonder: is it part of the show
this embarrassing wobbling,
this vain desperation to clutch?

Arraheids

See thon raws o flint arraheids
in oor gret museums o antiquities
awful grand in Embro –
Dae'ye near'n daur wunner at wur histrie?
Weel then, Bewaur !
The museums of Scotland are wrang.
They urnae arraheids
but a show o grannies' tongues,
the hard tongues o grannies
aa deid an gaun
back to thur peat and burns,
but for thur sherp
chert tongues, that lee
fur generations in the land
like wicked cherms, that lee
aa douce in the glessy cases in the gloom
o oor museums, an
they arenae lettin oan. but if you daur
sorn aboot an fancy
the vanished hunter, the wise deer runnin on;
wheesh . . . an you'll hear them,
fur they cannae keep fae muttering
ye arenae here tae wonder,
whae dae ye think ye ur?

Den of the old men

C'mon ye auld buggers, one by one
this first spring day, slowly down
the back braes with your walking sticks
and wee brown dugs, saying: *Aye, lass*
a snell wind yet but braw. Ye
half dozen relics of strong men
sat in kitchen chairs
behind the green gingham curtain

of yer den, where a wee dog grins
on last year's calender – we hear ye
clacking dominos the afternoon for pennies.
And if some wee tyke
puts a chuckie through the window
ye stuff yesterday's Courier
in the broken pane, saying
jails too guid fur them, tellys in cells!
– We can see your bunnets nod
and jaws move: what're ye up to
now you've your hut built,
now green hame-hammered benches
appear in the parish's secret soft-spots
like old men's spoor?
Is it carties? A tree-hoose?
Or will ye drag up driftwood;
and when she's busy with the bairns
remove your daughters' washing-lines
to lash a raft? Which,
if ye don't all fall out and argue
you can name the 'Pride o' Tay' and launch
some bright blue morning on the ebb-tide
and sail away, the lot of yez,
staring straight ahead
                    like captains
as you grow tiny
out on the wide Firth, tiny
as you drift past Ballinbreich, Balmurnie, Flisk
with your raincoats and bunnets,
                    wee dugs and sticks.

Xiahe

Abune the toon o Xiahe
a thrast monastery,
warn lik a yowe's tuith.

The sun gawps at innermaist

ingles o wa's.
Secret as speeders

folk hae criss-crosst a saucht
seedit i the yird flair
wi rags o win blawn prayer.

Xiahe. Wave droonin wave
on a pebbly shore,
the *ahe* o machair, o slammach,

o impatience; ahent the saft saltire
i trashed, an sheep;
wha's drift on the brae

is a lang cloud's shadda.
the herd cries a wheen wirds
o Tibetan sang,

an A'm waukenet, on a suddenty mindit:
A'm far fae hame,
I hae crossed China.

Xiahe *(pronounced Shi-ah-e) a Tibetan town in the now Chinese
province of Gansu;* sauch: *willow;* yird: *earth;* slammach: *cobweb.*

The way we live

Pass the tambourine, let me bash out praises
to the Lord God of movement, to Absolute
non-friction, flight, and the scarey side:
death by avalanche, birth by failed contraception.
Of chicken tandoori and reggae, loud, from tenements,
commitment, driving fast and unswerving
friendship. Of tee-shirts on pulleys, giros and Bombay,
barmen, dreaming waitresses with many fake-gold
bangles. Of airports, impulse, and waking to uncertainty,
to strip-lights, motorways, or that pantheon –

the mountains. To overdrafts and grafting

and the fit slow pulse of wipers as you're
creeping over Rannoch, while the God of moorland
walks abroad with his entourage of freezing fog,
his bodyguard of snow.
Of endless gloaming in the North, of Asiatic swelter,
to launderettes, anecdotes, passions and exhaustion,
Final Demands and dead men, the skeletal grip
of government. To misery and elation; mixed,
the sod and caprice of landlords.
To the way it fits, the way it is, the way it seems
to be: let me bash out praises – pass the tambourine.

Don Paterson

Don Paterson

❛ I was born in Dundee in 1963, and left school in 1980 to work as a sub for D.C. Thompson; I suddenly found it impossible to get up in the morning, and, to my enormous relief, was given my jotters after a few months. After that I began working as a jazz musician, something I still do. There's really no connection between the music I play and the poetry I write, and it would be a grave error if I tried to forge one. I moved to London in 1984, then Brighton in 1990, and at the moment I'm working as Writer-in-Residence at Dundee University.

Although I make scores of drafts for every poem, it's still pretty much an unconscious process, since at the time I'm only aware of thinking about the form, the rhythm, the syntax, how one word sits with another; I think matters of self-expression, the imagination, and style should be left to take care of themselves. They're not negotiable qualities – they're either there or not, and meddling with them tends to destroy the mysterious nature of the process; since that mystery is about the only tangible reward poetry has to offer, you have to keep it sacred, or try to.

As for all the other stuff, the politics and aesthetics of it all, well, I'm as interested in that side of things as anyone else; but since these discussions are invariably *post hoc* – that's to say they take place after the umbilicus between myself and the poem has been severed – I don't consider my own remarks to be any more relevant or interesting than anyone else's. This isn't so much humility as an abdication of responsibility; but too many poems these days anticipate the arguments they raise in the course of telling themselves. The most serious consequence of this extra-literary garbage creeping in is simply that the poem becomes less entertaining; and since a poem has to entertain and divert the reader before it can set its sights any higher, this is just about the worst thing that can happen. For me, bad poems try to offer solutions, while good poems leave a little more chaos, mystery, fear or wonder in the world than there was before. ❜

Publications:

Nil Nil (Faber, 1993) (PBS Choice)

The Trans-Siberian Express

(for Eva)

One day we will make our perfect journey –
the great train smashing through Dundee, Brooklyn
and off into the endless tundra,
the earth flattening out before us.

I follow your continuous arrival,
shedding veil after veil after veil –
the automatic doors wincing away
while you stagger back from the buffet

slopping *Laphroaig* and decent coffee
until you face me from that long enfilade
of glass, stretched to vanishing point
like facing mirrors, a lifetime of days.

Amnesia

I was, as they later confirmed, a very sick boy.
The star performer at the meeting house,
my eyes rolled back to show the whites, my arms
outstretched in catatonic supplication
while I gibbered impeccably in the gorgeous tongues
of the aerial orders. On Tuesday nights, before
I hit the Mission, I'd nurse my little secret:
Blind Annie Spall, the dead evangelist
I'd found still dying in creditable squalor
above the fishmonger's in Rankine Street.
The room was ripe with gurry and old sweat;
from her socket in the greasy mattress, Annie
belted through hoarse chorus after chorus
while I prayed loudly, absently enlarging
the crater that I'd gouged in the soft plaster.
Her eyes had been put out before the war,

just in time to never see the daughter
with the hare-lip and the kilt of dirty dishtowels
who ran the brothel from the upstairs flat
and who'd chap to let me know my time was up,
then lead me down the dark hall, its zoo-smell,
her slippers peeling off the sticky lino.
At the door, I'd shush her quiet, pressing
my bus-fare earnestly into her hand.

Four years later. Picture me: drenched in patchouli,
strafed with hash-burns, casually arranged
on Susie's bed. Smouldering frangipani;
Dali's *The Persistence of Memory*;
pink silk loosely knotted round the lamp
to soften the light; a sheaf of Penguin Classics,
their spines all carefully broken in the middle;
a John Martyn album mumbling through the speakers.
One hand was jacked up her skirt, the other trailing
over the cool wall behind the headboard
where I found the hole in the plaster again.
The room stopped like a lift; Sue went on talking.
It was a nightmare, Don. We had to gut the place.

An Elliptical Stylus

My uncle was beaming: 'Aye, yer elliptical stylus –
fairly brings out a' the wee details.'
Balanced at a fraction of an ounce
the fat cartridge sank down like a feather;
music billowed into three dimensions
as if we could have walked between the players.

My Dad, who could appreciate the difference,
went to Largs to buy an elliptical stylus
for our ancient, beat-up Phillips turntable.
We had the guy in stitches: 'You can't . . .
er . . . you'll have to *upgrade your equipment*.'
Still smirking, he sent us from the shop

with a box of needles, thick as carpet-tacks,
the only sort they made to fit our model.

(Supposing I'd been *his* son: let's eavesdrop
on 'Fidelities', the poem I'm writing now:
The day my father died, he showed me how
he'd prime the deck for optimum performance:
it's that lesson I recall – how he'd refine
the arm's weight, to leave the stylus balanced
somewhere between ellipsis and precision,
as I gently lower the sharp nip to the line
and wait for it to pick up the vibration
till it moves across the page, like a cardiograph . . .)

We drove back slowly, as if we had a puncture;
my Dad trying not to blink, and that man's laugh
stuck in my head, which is where the story sticks,
and any attempt to cauterize this fable
with something axiomatic on the nature
of articulacy and inheritance,
since he can well afford to make his *own*
excuses, you your own interpretation.
But if you still insist on resonance –
I'd swing for him, and every other cunt
happy to let my father know his station,
which probably includes yourself. To be blunt.

Sisters

(for Eva)

Back then, our well of tenements
powered the black torch that could find
the moon at midday: four hours later
the stars would be squandered on us.

*

As the sun spread on her freckled back

I felt as if I'd turned the corner
to a bright street, scattered with coins;
for weeks, I counted them over and over.

*

In a dark kitchen, my ears still burning,
I'd dump the lilo, binoculars, almanac
and close the door on the flourishing mess
of Arabic and broken lines.

*

Though she swears they're not identical
when I dropped her sister at the airport
my palms hurt as she spoke my name
and I bit my tongue back when I kissed her.

*

Nowadays, having shrunk the sky
to a skull-sized planetarium
– all fairy-lights and yawning voice-overs –
I only stay up for novae, or comets.

*

Some mornings I wake, and fantasize
I've slipped into her husband's place
as he breathes at her back, sliding his tongue
through Fomalhaut and the Southern Cross.

Nil Nil

*Just as any truly accurate representation of a particular geography
can only exist on a scale of 1:1 (imagine the vast, rustling map of
Burgundy, say, settling over it like a freshly-starched sheet!) so it
is with all our abandoned histories, those ignoble lines of succes-
sion that end in neither triumph nor disaster, but merely plunge on
into deeper and deeper obscurity; only in the infinite ghost-libraries
of the imagination – their only possible analogue – can their ends
be pursued, the dull and terrible facts finally authenticated.*
                              François Aussemain, *Pensées*

From the top, then, the zenith, the silent footage:
McGrandle, majestic in ankle-length shorts,
his golden hair shorn to an open book, sprinting

the length of the park for the long hoick forward,
his balletic toe-poke nearly bursting the roof
of the net; a shaky pan to the Erskine St End
where a plague of grey bonnets falls out of the clouds.
But ours is a game of two halves, and this game
the semi they went on to lose; from here
it's all down, from the First to the foot of the Second,
McGrandle, Visocchi and Spankie detaching
like bubbles to speed the descent into pitch-sharing,
pay-cuts, pawned silver, the Highland Division,
the absolute sitters ballooned over open goals,
the dismal nutmegs, the scores so obscene
no respectable journal will print them; though one day
Farquhar's spectacular bicycle-kick
will earn him a name-check in Monday's obituaries.
Besides the one setback – the spell of giant-killing
in the Cup (Lochee Violet, then Aberdeen Bon Accord,
the deadlock with Lochee Harp finally broken
by Farquhar's own-goal in the replay)
nothing inhibits the fifty-year slide
into Sunday League, big tartan flasks,
open hatchbacks parked squint behind goal-nets,
the half-time satsuma, the dog on the pitch,
then the Boy's Club, sponsored by Skelly Assurance,
then Skelly Dry Cleaners, then nobody;
stud-harrowed pitches with one-in-five inclines,
grim fathers and perverts with Old English Sheepdogs
lining the touch, moaning softly.
Now the unrefereed thirty-a-sides,
terrified fat boys with callipers minding
four jackets on infinite, notional fields;
ten years of dwindling, half-hearted kickabouts
leaves two little boys – Alastair Watt,
who answers to 'Forty', and wee Horace Madden,
so smelly the air seems to quiver above him –
playing desperate two-touch with a bald tennis ball
in the hour before lighting-up time.
Alastair cheats, and goes off with the ball
leaving wee Horace to hack up a stone
and dribble it home in the rain;
past the stopped swings, the dead shanty-town

of allotments, the black shell of Skelly Dry Cleaners
and into his cul-de-sac, where, accidentally,
he neatly back-heels it straight into the gutter
then tries to swank off like he meant it.

Unknown to him, it is all that remains
of a lone fighter-pilot, who, returning at dawn
to find Leuchars was not where he'd left it,
took time out to watch the Sidlaws unsheathed
from their great black tarpaulin, the haar burn off Tayport
and Venus melt into Carnoustie, igniting
the shoreline; no wind, not a cloud in the sky
and no one around to admire the discretion
of his unscheduled exit: the engine plopped out
and would not re-engage, sending him silently
twirling away like an ash-key,
his attempt to bail out only partly successful,
yesterday having been April the 1st –
the ripcord unleashing a flurry of socks
like a sackful of doves rendered up to the heavens
in private irenicon. He caught up with the plane
on the ground, just at the instant the tank blew
and made nothing of him, save for his fillings,
his tackets, his lucky half-crown and his gallstone,
now anchored between the steel bars of a stank
that looks to be biting the bullet on this one.

In short, this is where you get off, reader;
I'll continue alone, on foot, in the failing light,
following the trail as it steadily fades
into road-repairs, birdsong, the weather, nirvana,
the plot thinning down to a point so refined
not even the angels could dance on it. Goodbye.

Raymond Friel

‘ I was born in Greenock in 1963 and went to primary school there. At the age of eleven I decided that I wanted to be a priest, a fact which delighted my father. I was therefore given every encouragement in my vocation. Three seminaries later (two in Scotland, one in Ireland), at the age of nineteen, I gave up on priesthood, worked in hotels for a year and then went to Glasgow University, graduating in 1987. Since then I've lived in England and Wales and currently work as a teacher in a Sixth Form College in west London. I've had the sense of 'returning home', then, for going on twenty years.

Perhaps this explains what I consider to be the dominant tone in much of my writing, that of elegy. I experience this most strongly in relation to those two stern grandfathers who feature in many Scottish childhoods: class and religion. I was born into a community which defined itself as strictly Catholic in relation to the majority, and a broader community which was aware of itself as working class. Both provided stability and offered a clear, if narrow, vision of the world. My distance now from both is a source of much of what I write.

Recently, that sense of elegy has been provoked most strongly by the sudden death of shipbuilding in Greenock. A way of life, a livelihood, has been deliberately and unnecessarily destroyed: a sadly familiar story in many towns in Scotland which grew up around heavy industry. The poem 'Schooldays' tries to express my relationship with this experience. Although I was brought up in the east end of Greenock, downwind of the former mansions of Victorian shipping tycoons, the yards were not a part of my everyday domestic experience. Of my family, only my grandfather worked there and just a handful of my classmates from Primary school went on to become the last intake of apprentices at Scott Lithgow, and by then I had lost touch. The fact that I *am* in a classroom and not wedged up a chimney, is an indication of progress, but not a cause for complacency in these times when the values of comprehensive education are being eroded.

Class and religion: my imagination has been determined by these forces in ways I am only now finding the means to explore. My displacement and distance from both goads me into poetry, although the term poet is one which sits uneasily on my shoulders. W.S. Graham, a poet of international renown, from Greenock, before a reading one night in England, fuelled by a large intake of whisky, was suddenly seized by anxiety. 'What am I?' he asked friends who were encouraging him to go on and read, 'Am I a poet or am I just a boy from Greenock?' This anecdote strikes a chord deep within me. There is a reflex of self-doubt we have yet to unlearn. 〉

Publications:

Bel-Air (Southfields Press, 1993)

First Communion

Church bells doing their nut
In the brittle morning.
Fags lit deep in jackets.
A silver coin, cold in my palm.

Where's uncle Tommy gone?
Dabbed wetly round the mouth,
And shooshed from questions in-
to an air of solemnity:

The organ sonorous,
The altar bushed with flowers;
Miss Day: *For goodness sake
ENUNCIATE! Now after three* . . .

Grace danced was the chorus.
I didn't understand.
The plate dunted my throat;
The priest's hand, trembling; *amen.*

It tasted like paper.
*Now say your thanksgiving
Into yourself: Sweet Jesus* . . .
How did it go again?
                              Sweet Jesus . . .

Schooldays

A soaked-to-the-skin wait
In the motley tail-end
That made up the numbers,
Then told to go and defend.

My big news at tea-time
Was if I *got a kick* . . .

A short-lived toe-ender
In the goalmouth panic.

But some of them had style . . .
Chesting it down, past
One and angled in off the bin,
Raising a nonchalant fist.

A po-faced Miss Pinelli,
Clean page and today's date . . .
Hands aching to record
Some boozed-up empire's fate.

The projects, more fun,
Like The Industrial Age . . .
The Use of Child Labour
A stick boy on the page.

McCreary, the hard man,
Blurting out 'I hate this!'
Collared out to the front,
Still defiant, 'What *miss?*'

One time he called her a cow . . .
God, a scattering of chairs
As she flew after him out
The door to riotous cheers!

But dead comfy up the back,
I could usually retreat
Into pure vacancy and stare
Down at Cartsburn Street . . .

Where the heavy-booted men
Came drawn by the siren,
A shuffling procession
Into forests of iron.

Hogmanay

At the bells
We stood up stiffly
And tinged the cut crystal
To the new year.

Dad slipped off
To sprinkle the rooms
(And anyone in them)
With holy water.

Left in peace,
I breathed in
At the open window
Where the night used to be so full

Of ships' horns
Blasting the sky
With gargantuan flatulence;
Close encounters of the blurred kind.

Tonight though
Merely a sad pamp
Lingers a moment
Over the town.

Lights go out;
Somewhere the river
Wrinkles in the dark,
Prowling west.

The dead shift
Under its cold pelt,
Dulse-entangled.
They will not come back,

Transfigured
In half-lit, creepy tales.
We don't go in

So much for myths,

Believing more
Often than not,
That life's exactly
What it looks like.

The Working-Class Poet

Someone else had set the thing up.
Sue didn't have the time herself.
All the features editor said
was the Holiday Inn at 12
to meet some poet. Her research
was a bit thin. To hell with it.
a few drinks and she'd have enough.

She sat in the hotel lobby
with the finished bits and pieces
of coffee left on the table
at her knee. She smiled weakly back
at the porter and leant forward
to fold her cigarette into
extinction. 12:47.

One Less

Going out with her I remember
was like going out with fifty people.
All the time she talked about her mother,
whose mission in life was to get her married
into the right family. (The latest
was vetted for background and salary;
which bombed me right out – student. Catholic

and a one syllable Irish surname).
    She talked about her father, and her brothers;
and her grandmother, who listened to her;
    and her friends, of course, and her friend's boyfriends.
And *her* boyfriends; which was the worst of it.
    I never did get used to that, hearing
her discuss so-and-so and look at me
    as if I was to give an opinion.
That never seemed to bother her at all.
    It bothered me alright. I used to think
if she's telling me all this about them
    what do the rest of them know about me.
It was a different world. Anyway,
    the whole thing lasted about three months.
And when it was finally all over
    and I turned up at her flat for dinner
and told her, before she set the table,
    that I really thought we should finish it,
she was perfect – she called me a bastard
    and put a million and one foul curses
upon my life and future happiness
    and stormed about the room and slammed the door
and said I could bloody well starve then
    and cried and went and stood by the window.
Five minutes later she gave me a hug
    and made me promise we'd always be friends.
Sure. I left the flat and walked out into
    the beautiful, cool summer's evening,
    leaving her to it, giving her one less
to worry about, one less to worry.
    But there were I remember moments
when I felt alone with her and happy,
    when I fell for the whole bit –
taking a lazy walk in the twilight
    through Kelvingrove park, picking off the leaves,
at ease with each other, chatting away
    about nothing much in particular,
and she would give me a sideways look and smile,
    as if she knew exactly what that did to me.

Angela McSeveney

Angela McSeveney

❛ I was born in 1964 and brought up and educated in Scotland. I went to four primary schools – some of which I hated – and fell behind with the work, partly because I was short-sighted for several years before anyone discovered I needed glasses. Luckily I was able to see close up so although the blackboard was a blur and I was awful at ballgames I could still read books and comics. I was bullied at school and bored stiff in class so I think that's why I enjoyed reading – the sheer escapism.

I was nine when I started to write stories for myself; I think it was another form of escapism. I read *We Didn't Mean To Go To Sea* by Arthur Ransome and enjoyed it so much that I began to write a novel of my own the next day.

I didn't have much paper so scrounged most of it by tearing out the flyleaves of all the books I could find in the house. (I still cringe when I remember vandalising a huge physiology text book that belonged to my oldest sister).

When I was ten I moved to a school I liked and got some glasses. Things improved a lot after that: I was never any use at sport but at least I didn't fall over so often.

I kept on writing stories and also began to write poetry when I was about fourteen. I pushed myself hard at Secondary School to make up for the days when I was blind as a bat and bottom of the class. I was at Edinburgh University 1982–86: I found it very hard going but got a degree on the second attempt. I took a class in Scottish Literature during my last year; to this day I regret that I only studied it for a year and took so long to find it.

I now write only poetry. In general I don't search out subjects, I just let ideas happen – a metaphor, one phrase, a reflection – and everything else grows from there. I don't have any plans beyond whatever poem I'm working on. I want the poems to be straightforward; to be understood after just a couple of readings at the most.

When I was a child I suppose I wrote for the same reasons that children draw or play with plasticine. I became more ambitious as I got older and by the time I left school I did hope to be published. ❜

Publications:

Poems in Other Tongues (Verse, 1990)
Coming Out With It (Polygon, 1992)

The Lump

Rolling over in a hot June night
I cradled my breasts in my arms
and felt a hard knot of tissue.

I was fifteen.
My life rose up in my throat
and threatened to stifle me.

It took three attempts to tell my mother.
She promised that my appointment would be
with a woman doctor.

A nurse called my name.
I didn't have cancer.

The stitches in my skin reminded me
of a chicken trussed for the oven.

I felt ashamed
that the first man to see me
had only been doing his job.

For The Best

I don't doubt you did it for the best.

After all I was twenty –
about time somebody did.

One of us was old enough to be my father,
the other to have known better.

I never said the word frigidity
– only went cold with the fear of it.

You rubbed me up the wrong way
and knowing that I must make the best of it.

The Fat Nymphomaniac's Poem

Tall men turn me on.
An immense man makes me petite and feminine.

For him I'm so much less the cow in a china shop.
My rugby tackle won't send him flying.

If there's more of him pound for pound
I can lay me down not smothering anyone.

Colin

Colin presided at my first tutorial,
read sex into all the symbolism,
told the tutor where to get off.

He wore striped trousers and pied shirts,
spoke of love being made in the room next to his.

To catch his glance made me blush.

We shared classes again in our second last term.
I wore pink dungarees at the front of the class.

Colin sat behind me in a herringbone coat
and took Jane Austen very seriously indeed.

Changing A Downie Cover

First: catch your downie.

They're big animals, sleep a lot of the time,
barely stirring as they snooze endlessly
loafing around on the beds.

But they only have to see
a clean cover –

suddenly you have six by three
of feathery incorporeality kicking and screaming
in your hands.

Wrestle them to the floor
and kneel on their necks:
you can't hurt them, no bones to break.

Pushing their head into the bag
keeps them quiet

but you're never sure
till each corner is flush inside the cover
securely buttoned shut.

They give up after that.
Pinioned in floral print polycotton
they lie back down and sleep.

The Bed And Breakfasts

They beamed into our lives
from nowhere –
one night stands on their Highland holidays.

Such exotica

when a carful arrived from America.

Enthroned in the sitting-room with the piano, best sofa,
the bed and breakfasts relished
fresh-laid eggs, homegrown vegetables.

My infantile craft,
hanging on the garden gate as they drove away,
was usually good for sixpence.

Only once
did anything come back to us
from their faraway imagined countries
– a packet of photos from Holland.

My sisters wear sensible shoes, print dresses.
I'm a toddler with hair curled like wood shavings.

Perhaps those children still smile from a Dutch album:
memories of a twenty years ago holiday?
quaint anthropological studies?

Less than a year later it all changed.
Dad worked in a factory,
we lived in a new town.

Night Shift

I would wake up when I heard Dad
coming in at the front door.

The others slept through his early morning noises:
a toilet flush, one cup of tea boiling.

There seemed no place for him
at home all day Saturday
and most of Sunday.

His skin paled
apart from one weather-beaten patch
at his throat.

'It's no life for a man,' he sometimes grumbled
'this living like a mole.'

During school holidays I made
no noise at home.

Mum went to parents' night alone.
She was sick of darning where industrial acid
ate away his clothes.

At five o'clock I'd be sent
to waken Dad for tea.

The curtains in my parents' room
were almost always closed.

The Pictures

To avoid distracting the workers
the mill windows were set in the roof.

Consequently my mother never saw sense
in spending an evening in the cinema
with no air and not even light.

But she did go to see *Gone With The Wind*
when it first came out.

It was the same day Bessie Henderson's hair
caught in her loom and she was scalped.

The men came running
but they were no use, fainting and going on.

A woman had to hold Bessie up
while an engineer cut her loose.
The worst of it was she didn't faint.

Bessie should have been one of the girls
who went to see *Gone With The Wind*.

My mother tried
but she couldn't like it much.

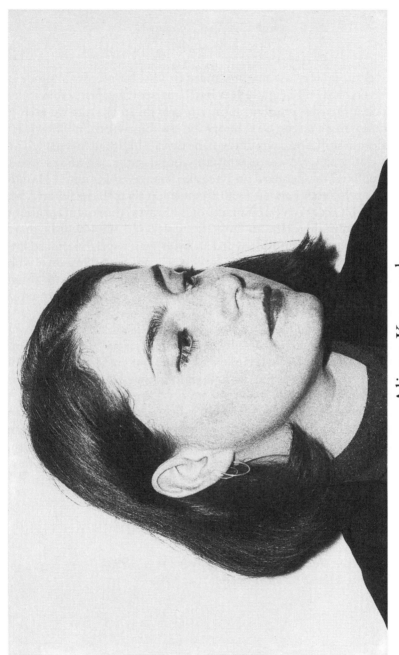

Alison Kermack

Alison Kermack

❝ah like plane wi wurdz.
thatz how ah rite.

av rittin poyitry aw ma life, mare ur less, bit ah nivvir shode it
tay naybiddy till a cupply yeer back. maisty it wiz pritty shite enny
rode, pritenshis crap. problim wiz see, thi sorty stuff we goat it
skule, ah thoat poyitry hudty be aw big wurdz n flowry hy
falootin stuff, so ah wiz kindy trine tay rite like that an it jist wizny
me. ah wizny reely sane whit ah wontid. latur oan ah discuvurt
foak like Tom Leonard an Ntozake Shange an Margaret Hamil-
ton an Manuel Bandeira nah thoat fuk, this iz thi reel wurld, ah
ken whit theez foak ur oan aboot. ah startid thinkin mare aboot
thi langwij hyrarky an how itz dafty say wun wurdz mare
impoartint thin anuthir wurd ur wun way i speekinz mare im-
poartint thin anuthir wy an how it wiz aw rilatid tay sane wun
persinz mare impoartint thin anuthir persin. like yi wurny aloud
tay tok aboot litrichur unless yi cood yooz big wurdz, which iz
nonsins uv coarse.

ah get loadzy ideaz fur poyumz jist by lisnin tay foak in barz
an caffyz an that. foak ur olwaze sane reelly amayzin poetic stuff,
ixpressin reelly hyooj complex ideaz inna singul sentins, jist in thi
coarsy a convursayshin. itz brillyint, thi hole lahgwij thing. thatz
how ah luv ritin say much. itz no olwaze good rite inuff. ah get
daze when ah dinny ken whit thi fuk am oan aboot an daze when
uthir foak tell mi *thay* dinny ken whit thi fuk am oan aboot an
daze when ah rite a loady shite an daze when ah dinny rite atoll,
eevin thoah wonty. jenrilly speekin itz jist sumthin ah needty day.
ah rite coz ah hufty. beein publishd iz an ucayshinil boanus. ❞

Publications:

Restricted Vocabulary (Clocktower Press, 1991)
Writing Like a Bastard (Rebel Inc, 1993)

Saltire

when ah wiz it skule
thur wiz loatsy flagz
oan thi frunty wur
Text Books

anna olwaze thot
it wiz thi teechur
hud pit a croass
throo thi scoattish wun

The Shadow Minister

by meenzy a contrapshun
like a perryscoap
wi a tellyscoap
attachd tay it
while cashully stroalin
aloang downin street
ah chansd tay look
in thi uppur windy
i nummer ten

ah seen thi pee em
sittin inna big arrum chare
in frunty a big coal fyur
hoaldin a mappy scoatlin
oan thi endy a toast foark

funny thing wiz
thoah kidny see it say cleerly
kizzit happind tay faw
oan thi oappisit waw
thi shaddy i thi pee em
wiz dane igzackly
thi same thing

Ikariss

it wiz hardur tay buleev in
upwurd mubility
when thay pit barbed wire
oan toappy thi lectric fens
thit ran roon thi skeem

Patriotic Pish

sumhow kinnectid
tay thi wottur supply
fur thi holy
thi cuntry

this yoorinul
in thi housy
commin lavvy

whare three pollytishuns
ur pishin

three streemzy pish
wun bloo
wun red
wun white

an thi puddil
killectin
roon thi drane
a yoonyin
jack

Askinfurrit

ah wiz reedin
in thi paipur
sum articul
aboot thi latist dibate
oan whit iz
an whit izny
rape
when thi doarbell went

ah oapind thi doar
an thi gy
standin thare sayz
yes?

ah sayz
wate a minnit
yoo rang thi bell

he sayz
yoo oapind thi doar
whidjy wont?

Time and Again

thi cloak
oan thi waw
sezitz timety

get thi bairnz reddy
get thi hoose tidy
get thi messijis in
get thi tee oan

get inty bed
an gee um hiz conjuggles

thur wizza time when
I

naw thur wizny

Richard Price

Richard Price

❝ I was born in Berkshire in 1966, but flitted with my parents to Renfrewshire when I was only six weeks old. The variousness of Renfrewshire is a bed-rock of my work. The heavy industries of car-building, ship-building and tanning there painfully gave way to electronics and computer manufacturers when I was growing up. That transition, and the co-existence of old and new implied by the suburbia and housing schemes typically built round weaving villages, saints' towns, and bridge settlements, the still-rural rivers and burns of the county, its effective annexation of Glasgow!, are riches which have deeply influenced my poems – in content and outlook.

I left school when I was sixteen to study journalism at Napier College in Edinburgh. Then I went to Strathclyde University where I studied English and librarianship. In 1988 I moved to London to work at the British Library. The dynamism of London, and the removal of its democratic forum in the 1980s, make it in some ways much more like Scotland than you might normally think. Partly as a result of those unexpected connections I had begun to make, in 1989 I approached W.N. Herbert with the idea of editing a magazine which would bring Scottish literature and ideas to the world: *Gairfish* began.

Writing about London, most extensively in *Tube Shelter Perspective*, has been a process of drawing attention to the issues of peripheralisation which are shared across many of the diverse cultures living in the 'United' Kingdom, but because London was also the place where I fell in love (Reader, I married her!), the city has been something of an accomplice in my love poetry. Songmakers first inspired me to write and still do; the lyric sensibility is strong in my work.

Edwin Morgan has been the most important Scottish poet for me. Neil M. Gunn has been the most important novelist. His books are often about finding 'luck', about wonderment, and about looking after those who are not lucky: I think there is a similar strand in my poetry. I tend to write taut, free verse with assonance, internal and tumbling rhymes. Exhilaration and fun seem to flow from freer forms, but satire, moments of poignance and a whole range of emotions are, I hope, possible. ❞

Publications:

The Fabulous Matter of Fact: the Poetics of Neil M. Gunn
(Edinburgh University Press, 1991)
Sense and a Minor Fever (Vennel Press, 1993)
Tube Shelter Perspective (Southfields Press, 1993)

forthcoming

An Informationist Primer (anthology) (with W.N. Herbert)
(Southfields Press, 1994)

Tree-bird

I'm lending you this poem –
it's yours.

Do you remember the owl-hawk, white as a guiser –
the dusk's sucky blanket tucked round our caravan
and the bird rid of us

like, at break-ripe, the fruit of the tree-bird tree,
the applefist which splits
into a beak and feathers,
a yellow tern
before Newton can say
Golden Delicious.

(It's a legend, you know, among fishers
who ken damn few trees
and they all shrubbery –
in this world, geese crack out of barnacles,
crabs lisp, and jellyfish are wedding veils
for mermaids who've vetoed
shivering grooms
in the wide aisle of a low ebb.)

I want to be the bird that's my hand in your hand,
to be the osprey that can dismember itself
like the lines of a poem,
climb the sky, dive, fish
and come back to itself
like a trick,
like the end of work.

With is

To ravel with you in ripening light.
To worry and adore

the stacking cups of your spine.

What I come with
is a dubious country,
a prejudice against people like us:
nationals who've dropped to couples,
two martens agog
under a tired Scots pine.

Our table is empty,
a summer curling pond.
Come on out on the town!
I've the nightbus map you lent me
when I was only a Scot.

Hinges

On the airstrip: fog.
Nothing taking off.
Five in the afternoon,
more or less.

I'd have called it a 'flitting'
but it was a year before I was born –
to my father it was 'moving house.'
He was Ma's envoy in Scotland:
he'd just chosen a field
that would grow into a bungalow
and he'd pay for it
whenever the bathroom,
opening on the hall
with a frosted glass door,
trapped her, towelnaked,
before the postman
and something to be signed for.

Through the same melted glass
I saw my first memory:

my eldest brother, nine or ten,
was stretching and not touching anything,
petrolburns on his face and hands,
a human X at the front door
(on a building site a friend
had clicked him alight;
we still don't know the bet).

On the airstrip: fog, night.
Eleven o'clock. My father is being practical
on the hotel phone: 'I am speaking
back in my room.'

In the morning in England, like a new couple
two police officers stood back
as Ma opened the door.
They had to be reassured:
she gave them tea in the fine bone.
(Just beyond the wicker of radar
the first plane out, just past midnight,
had dropped like a figurine.)

In the afternoon
my mother met my father in Arrivals.
Before they held held held each other
he says they shook hands.

At ease

Scotland hits eighty in May.

An electric mower blows its nose.
The explaining murmur is my father by the ladders;
the MacMillan visitor, months into this
conversation,
is at ease.

With my shirt off, everything is ridiculous:

dad in shorts and people in the wrong places.
Inside, like church, when mum says garden
she means an English one.

My father's record collection

The hard black Corryvreckan
is static.
All the blues are quiet
in the white-washed attic.

There's a dead shining black,
a brittle hour.
Between Beethoven and Broadway,
a pressed black flower.

Roddy Lumsden

❛ I started with poetry at seventeen in St Andrews, where I was born in 1966 and grew up. At Edinburgh University, writers-in-residence sanded me down and encouraged me to keep on. I'm sure that I'm not the only writer here to come through this way, and I hope cuts will not continue to affect writers-in-residence in further education and councils.

In 1991, I was summoned to the long table at the Society of Authors in Chelsea where the panel gave me an Eric Gregory Award. These are given annually to poets under thirty who show potential. Part of the money funded a month in New York City where I read my work round the open readings in Downtown Manhattan.

Most of my work seems to be about those old favourites euphumised as wine, women and song. Someday, I suppose I'll be writing about marriage, mortgage and misery, but I'm desperate to stretch out my already elongated youth a little longer.

My writing often focuses on the problems thrown up by human nature – how friendships come and go, how people fail to communicate – and I try to deal with what are 'men's problems' in the way that some women poets have addressed their specific dilemmas.

I write in many styles, often using rhyme and/or metre which fewer younger poets seem to be comfortable with. I like to mix lyrical language with modern idioms and 'buzzwords'. English is the world's richest language and is constantly evolving, adopting new words from the street and elsewhere.

'The Misanthrope's Afternoon Walk' is not typical of my work. It's half me-on-a-bad-day, and half in character. I like the idea of misanthropy being 'politically correct' because you detest everyone equally. A few of the words are my own. Other phrases are left ambiguous for the reader to chew over (what are daytime Valkyries or pale Sallys?).

In 'Detox', I was thinking of the necessity of facing up to disappointment and the strange, filmic pleasure that often accompanies this. 'Black Coffee' and 'I'll Get By' are old songs. ❜

The Misanthrope's Afternoon Walk

They're all out today.

The victims. The chipped on the shoulder.

The chipped on the cheek, the scarred.

Twinsets. Colonels. Lumps in leggings.

The mental cripples. Baby mothers,

Repros, pit bulls, shrunken dummy-suckers,

Bad-moustached shouldn't-have-been fathers.

Some shithorse in a kilt. A braindeath

In a security cap. Up-herself bitch

Who's taken Eve's apple rectally. Doctors

With skinrash. Checkout girls with threadworm.

The sane. The sober. Things that ought

To crawl. Bleeders. Greyhairs, pinkhairs,

Bluestockings. Old women whose ankles

You could splinter with a rabbit punch.

The cheer-up-son recalcitrant I'd

Dearly love to spine. Other things up

For overdue skinning. Ne'er-do-wells.

Existant traumas. Bed wetters. Kleptos.

Bores at the bar. Ratracers, boy racers.

The pierced, the tattooed, the body haired.

Those on necessary medication. Bored

Mother, prammed sprog. The disarranged,

Arranged married. Programmed. AAs.

TTs, TAs, SoBs. Clearance orphans.

Door openers. Little whistlers. Bograds.

Pick a cards. Toe rags. They're out.

Advocates. Recidivists. Tourrets,

Twitchers, fornicators. Random attackers,

Poisoners of baby food and cat killers.

They're all out. The ineffectual.

Hitler faces, Sutcliffe faces. Showbiz

Lookalikes. Household pimps, home breakers.

Tragic circumstance. Greens eaters, face

Painters, crystal gazers, got-the-plans-in-a

Drawer-somewhere. The superstitious.

The witless camp who's draining

His drag queen's resources. The other

Resourceless many. The hang-at-the-door.

Pigeon fanciers. Narks. Original sinners.

Down and outers you might hammer

To a cross. Tell-tale-tits. Boozers.

They're out. Cathartics. Valium

Swallowing lost-it-years-backs, drying out.

Hangers over the fence. Natterers.

The victims. The challenged. The child

Bride. Carlins, bauchles and bodachies.

The hobbledehoy and the gran bene mort,

Arm in withered arm. He who's always there,

And will be, hand out, until he's washed

Up in three black sacks. Termagants from

The Class of Nineteen Oatcake. Mousies,

Cloppers, clumphers, the incompetent.

Mobsters, poor ones at that. Secretaries.

Bedroom centrefolders, drains, Little Nells,

Spunkrags. Pale Sallys signing any scrap.

Hen-hearted primps. All hell's broiled family.

Fee-paying wantons. Daytime Valkyries.

They're out walking. Drastic short stories

You can't wait to reach the end of.

Candle

Whose tether are you at the end of?
Not the dozing lovers,
A dozen to a block down Clerk Street,
For whom you're the last of many lights.

And dripping with fear? What makes you think
Your life need be so short?
Multiplied by memory, you'll surely be
A Methuselah amongst appliances.

Like all things, like the bottle you're planted in,
It's not those looks that count.
You're on function. I've forgiven
Your pallid lack of the aesthetic.

You're good at playing piggy-in-the-middle
Tonight, I wonder what it is
That fails to show its face
At that other side of you.

You're showing off that black triangle
Where my finger would not burn.
And yet you hide the void above your tip
Where death might start.

The only thing that's burning
In this house right now is you.
Sleep calling, it's my jealousy
Which sneaks up and blows you out.

Detox

5 p.m. Mister Halfmast, I kick my
Mind toward the blues. Black
Coffee. I'll Get By. Whatever.

If you walked in on me, you'd
Find me flinching, drawing
Out the needle of my worst thought.

It's a picture that's lacking
A soundtrack. Go get me one
With a smoky sax, with a good dose

Of steel-brushed cymbals. Then,
On the way back, red wine,
Two bottles, some French cigarettes.

Sit on the floor and look me over.
Tell me I'll be okay. Then,
Get the hell out of here. Now.

Don't you see I'm the star of
This scene? Let me finish
This thing I didn't want to start.

Stuart A. Paterson

Stuart A. Paterson

❛ I was born in Truro in 1966 but have lived in Ayrshire since 1970 when my family returned north. Hope to complete a degree in English at Stirling in 1995; worked as storeman, creeler, dishwasher, landscape gardener and cook before returning to FE in 1987. Wrote verse with any seriousness since age of twenty-three. Work published in various reviews in Britain and abroad. Winner of an Eric Gregory Award in 1992, and received a SAC Writer's Bursary in 1993. Admire the poetry of MacDiarmid, Housman, Conn, Neill, among others. Active SNP member, kind to cats and live by the Ayrshire coast, but not at present. . . .

I can explain certain reasons for wanting to write about certain subjects, I can explain why I have a preference for writing in 'traditional' poetic forms. Overall, though, I couldn't cohesively put into spoken or written word the essential need which compels me to write – writing verse/poetry/whatever has always been a natural occurrence for me. Perhaps, after all, poets are 'born' not 'made'. Though this might sound unnecessarily grand, it's the only explanation I can find which, for me, goes some way to explaining why I put into verse and not art or song, my joy at Jim Watt winning the world boxing championship when I was thirteen, my despair at Kilmarnock nosediving to Division One when I was seventeen, my failures with the opposite sex (still happening 'and how I wish I could sing the blues instead of blether in verse about it, at such times').

Being born of 'guid Ayrshire stock' and raised in a household where braid Scots was the norm, and an ominously guttural saying put me firmly in place or a bairn-rhyme lulled me to sleep when younger – the use of lyrical, poetic language was always around me. Although writing mostly in English, I believe that rhythm and musicality of Scots has carried over in such a way as to mark it distinctly as 'Scottish'. I like to write in forms which these days seem to be cynical and academic, but I hold the belief that obscurity and contemporaneity seldom stand the test of time, and that, also, well-written poetry will communicate through the years, societies and fashions. Poetry should not be the mind-monopoly of a contemporary intellectual few, but should have the ability to transcend class and culture, however these are defined. So, I will keep writing, keep searching (as I think all writers do) for that ultimate line-sequence, keep acting on sudden spurs and ideas which laxate the mind at all hours of day and night and try not to reason out the 'whys' to the detriment of the 'whats' – let others do that if they can be bothered. ❜

A Rush of Memory by Polmaise

At eleven I kissed the neighbourhood sweetheart,
Twelve she was, a stoneless peach then, furless
And ripe from the bough. It was a slap
Of wet concentration and closed eyes, tongueless
In the innocence of elevenishness and in
The spidery lair of a bin cupboard during
A preparatory dare for the coming school day.

At fifteen I kissed my first girlfriend,
Seventeen she was, a hairy rootmonger of men
All tousled from unmade beds. It was a suck
With a pull like a vacuum-cleaner. Tongueless
No more she forced the safety of my lips,
Seemed like she wanted my tonsils for a souvenir,
Welding our mouths with glue. I gargled later.

At sixteen I kissed my first love
For a whole three months, she was blond and frail
The way that kewpies are. It was summer,
And once I lay on top of her, in a field, young,
Hard as a hill, the dog's head cocked, no longer
Hoovering flies. If we'd gone one day
Without seeing each other we'd have died.

At seventeen I kissed a date ON THE TIT!
Twenty-one she was, immensely-nippled, almost
(But not quite) able to feed me, suckling, snorting away.
Mouths were irrelevant as we freed them to grab at
The mysterious sculpting and folds of flesh.
I tried to kiss her goodnight one time, she laughed
And groped me. Kissing was never the same.

At twenty-two I kissed a girl, cold dry
Funeral of love at a bus-stop, our first kiss,
One of farewell from two kindred souls
Who never dared broach the borders of cloth
Yet held hands for comfort in a friendless world.
As I watched her go, my lips hung open to reveal

A tongue for talking. Kissing was learning to speak.

Not long ago, skinned of promises,
I kissed a girl near a ruined castle, shaded
By majesty of sequoia, drawn to cool stone,
Lapped by water, wing, the essential solitude of kisses.

Fife

Dappled moorings by the grey
return to canvases in
Edinburgh antique shops showing
Crail or Kingsbarns in 1800.

The net-boys by the catch
smile, unaware, a legacy.
Low-slung harbour cottages
reek years away. Old crewmen,

worn by salt-spray, on
the breaking wall sniff for
lobster cooked wailing
on a high flame, watching

young ones lowered to boats.
City-dwellers on an open sea
of calm harbour shriek
camcorder laughs for Castlemilk.

Beyond walk more tourists
over dry cobbles, snapping
at the small auctions of lives
like a shoal of fat halibut.

Each day the spray is colder,
just a little grimier. Each
morning sees another wrinkle
frame a sun-caught smile.

The Leaving of Scotland

News at Ten,
January 1st 1997.

The news breaks on the eve of another
Border-summit, Scotland has asked for

Political asylum from Parliament Square.
They're putting up fences and putting out fires

In Motherwell, chaining the trawlers to
Each other in Fraserburgh as black-clad

Fish-terrorists riot and threaten a cod
War with Iceland, rushing the Secretary

Of State to a live TV broadcast in
Glasgow where, it's been reported, red

Kelvinsiders are demanding a
Fortune for Pat Lally's release from the

National Concert Hall. Poets are marching
To Fergusson's statue on the Mound singing

Venceramos, keeping police at bay with
Metaphors for educational cut-backs

In *Sabhal Mor Ostaig*. University
Students in Dundee are demanding the release

Of Douglas Dunn from a police cell in London
Where, in a *Scottish Books Special* emergency

Broadcast from the South Bank Centre, he
Called for the reintegration of

Scottish regiments. The news has broken,
Ayrshire has declared its independence

And littered the road to Glasgow with glass.
Up north, an organisation

Of Aberdeen radicals calling itself
The Scottish Offshore Republican Army

Has captured an oil rig in the name of
Ravenscraig. The Military are making a

Giant jail of the Highlands, repopulation
Of the Islands has begun and Gaelic

Is compulsory, English forbidden,
The Daily Record has barricaded itself

By the Broomielaw and blamed it all on
Dissatisfied Mirror Group Pensioners

In collusion with the Scottish Office.
Michael Forsyth has returned and instituted

A four-year plan for dissident writers
When it's discovered that 'Mac' is old Pictish

For 'comrade of'. McLeod, McLean,
MacIlvanney (and Massie for the sake of it)

Are rounded up to work crofts on only sixteen pounds
Each a week, deliver the mail, start spinning new cottage

Industries, teach their children the Works of
Walter Scott and Teatime Tales by Molly Weir.

All over Scotland, town halls
Are giving out free paper and copies of

Dwelly's English-Gaelic Dictionary.
The Herald has made Tom Shields Editor

And called for Pat Lally's release but his
Corpse is thrown from the roof of the Concert

Hall an hour later, tidied, bewigged
And flown to an all-expenses-paid

Funeral junket in Chicago.
The border-summit breaks up again,

No sign of agreement on extradition
For convicted heroin smugglers,

I'm sorry, I'll read that again,
convicted *herring* smugglers.

English embassies, packed with Inverness
Publicans and time-share owners, appeal

To the European Community for help.
But the oil's run out and so has Scotland.

Political asylum denied, it leaves.

Dream State

a country so awake that
dreaming is for the sleepless,
but I think a back-here-then

when you'd maybe catch a fox
ear-deep in rubbish most
mornings, raking through full bins

for bones, *fragranta vesca*
honeying a hard soil in
new June, small tender fruits

for mouths yet too soft to take
ribes sylvestre's sharp blood
and tell-tale stain, football cards

in nationally-arranged piles
on the mantelpiece, Dalglish
and Keegan good company

one-dimensionally, food
like stovies, kedgeree, plain
but Scottish delights; to our young

lapping tongues, a nationalism
of proteins, a huge country
of undiscovered tastes

to fill the thoughts of small heads
put to bed before their world grew,
flag rose, fox came raking through

our back yard, when you'd maybe
catch the dream state long before
it woke to morning's red sky

laid along the contours of
a massive upset dustbin
someone ransacked while we slept.

Anne C. Frater

Anne C. Frater

❛ I was born in Stornoway in 1967 and brought up in Upper Bayble on the Isle of Lewis. I went to school in Bayble and at the Nicolson Institute in Stornoway, before leaving Lewis to study at Glasgow University in 1985. I graduated with an honours degree in Celtic and French in 1990, and went on to gain a teaching diploma from Jordanhill College. I returned to Glasgow University in 1991, where I am at present working towards a Ph.D in Gaelic.

My feelings for my first language, Gaelic, and my despair at the thought of its decline is the motivation for much of my poetry, although the pictures I paint nowadays are not quite as gloomy as those of my first poetic efforts: I just hope that the Gaelic revival has not come too late to halt the decline. I have been a Scottish Nationalist for as long as I can remember, so naturally this is easily seen in my work. I honestly do not believe that Scotland will have the kind of government to suit the needs of its people until that government is from Edinburgh rather than Westminster, and I cannot understand those who continue to put their faith in English-based political parties. Much of my poetry is very personal, dealing with people I know, or situations in which I have been, although I have to admit that not all the unrequited love poems are based on personal experience: one or two have been inspired by letters to problem pages! Having said that, in the majority of those depressing poems, the sad creature concerned *is* me.

I do not set out to ask questions in my poetry, but to look at situations in a different way, and to tie them in to other themes. I like to use allegorical images in order to get my message across, rather than to just baldly state my point of view. I hope that my poetry now and again makes people stop and think a little. ❜

Publications:

Poems have appeared in

An Aghaidh na Siorraidheachd/ In the Face of Eternity (Polygon, 1990)
An Anthology of Scottish Women Poets (EUP, 1991)
Siud an Eilean/ There Goes the Island (Acair, 1993)

Bàs na h-Eala

Thog thu ar dòchas air sgiathan eala,
gheall thu dhuinn uile làithean geala –
agus a-nis tron cheathach
tha thu a' seasamh mar thaibhs'
fliuch falamh san uisge
mar chailleach aosda a thug beatha
do iomadh duine na tìde.
Ach a-nis tha do bhroinn falamh
tha do chlann air d' fhàgail
agus tha do làithean cruthachaidh seachad.

Lit' gun Shalainn

Sgian dubh na stocainn
agus Beurla na bheul;
moladh lit' sa mhadainn
's e cur muesli na bhòbhl;
'Chan fhaighear nas fheàrr na 'n t-uisge-beatha.'
Ach 's e Martini bhios e 'g òl . . .
Nach ann truagh a tha 'n cluaran
le boladh an ròis!

The Death of the Swan

You raised our hopes on the wings of a swan
you promised us all brighter days –
and now, through the mist
you stand like a wraith,
wet and empty in the rain
like an old woman who in her time
gave her life to many;
but now your womb is empty,
your children have left you
and your fertile days have gone.

Unsalted Porridge

A *sgian dubh* in his stocking
and English on his tongue;
praising porridge in the morning
as he puts muesli in his bowl;
'You can't get better than whisky.'
But it's Martini that he drinks . . .
Isn't the thistle pitiful
when it smells of the rose!

9mh den t-Samhainn 1989

Danns' air a'bhalla . . .
Casan saor a' cluich puirt
air clachan cruaidh,
's a' uèir-ghathach air a lomadh
le bualadh nam bas . . .
No man's land
loma-làn le daoine
's iad a' dol seachad air Teàrlach –
chan ann gun fhiost
ach gun sgrùdadh –
agus na càirdean a' feitheamh
le gàire nan gàirdean . . .
agus gàir' aig na gàrdan
's gun fheum ac' air gunna
airson bacadh a thogail agus blocan a leagail . . .
Cailleach a' tighinn
gu geata Bhrandenburg,
nach eil fhathast air fhosgladh
cho farsaing ri càch,
saighdear òg a' dol thuice
's i a' seasamh, gu daingeann
's a' coimhead a slighe
mar cheunmannan ceadachaidh
na chlàr fo a casan,
ga slaodadh,
ga tarraing,
's i gluasad a-rithist,
's a' coimhead an òigeir,
's a' toirt dùbhlan dha
a tilleadh air ais.
Làmh air a gualainn,
greim air a h-uilinn,
's i gun chothrom
a dhol an aghaidh a' churaidh
bha ga stiùireadh dìreach
gu Brandenburg,
gu teampall a saorsa . . .

9th November 1989

Dancing on the wall . . .
Feet freely playing tunes
on hard stones,
the barbed wire made smooth
by the beating of hands . . .
No man's land
brimming over with people
as they pass Charlie –
not furtively
but without scrutiny –
and their friends wait
with a smile in their arms . . .
and the guards laugh,
as they need no guns
to lift barriers
and knock down bricks . . .
An old woman comes
to the Brandenburg Gate,
which is not yet open
as wide as the rest,
a young soldier goes to her
and she stands firm
looking at her path
laid out at her feet
like steps of permission,
pulling her,
drawing her,
and she moves again,
and she watches the youth
daring him
to turn her back.
A hand on her shoulder,
a grip on her elbow,
and she is powerless
to resist the brave
who leads her straight
to Brandenburg,
to her temple of freedom . . .

A-raoir
gun imcheist
bhiodh e air peilear a chur innt'.

Smuain

'Alba saor no na fàsach.'
Saorsa no gainmheach
canaidh iad ruinn an aon rud:
'Gheibh sibh sin . . .
ach cumaidh sinne an ola.'

Dà rathad

Carson a bu chòir dhomh gabhail
na slighe ceart, lom, fada?
Ged a tha an rathad air a bheil mi cam
agus tha na clachan a' gearradh mo chasan,
agus tha dìreadh an leòthaid
gam fhàgail gun anail,
chan e an aon rud
a tha mise coimhead romham
latha an dèidh latha.
Agus shuas air an leathad
chì mi timcheall orm,
chì mi gu bheil barrachd ann dhòmhs'
na slighe cheart, fhada, lom.
Tha thusa cumail do shùilean air an aon rud
ceart, dìreach air do bheulaibh –
agus chan fhaic thu gu bheil an saoghal
ag atharrachadh timcheall ort.

Last night
without hesitation
he would have shot her.

A Thought

'Scotland free or a desert'.
Freedom or sand
they'll say the same thing to us:
'You can have that . . .
but we'll keep the oil.'

Two Roads

Why should I follow
the long, smooth, straight road?
Although the road I take is crooked
and the stones cut my feet
and climbing the hill
leaves me breathless
I am not confronted
by the same prospect
day after day.
And up on the hill
I can see around me,
I can see that there is more in store for me
than a straight, long, smooth road.
You keep your eyes fixed on one point
right in front of you –
and you cannot see
that the world is changing around you.

Aig an Fhaing

Nam sheasamh thall aig geat a' phrèiridh,
feur glan fom bhòtannan,
làmhan fuar nam phòcaidean,
fàileadh an dup
gu fann
gu neo-chinnteach
a' nochdadh mu mo chuinnlean
's mi a' coimhead càch cruinn
lachanaich le chèile
timcheall air an fhaing:
a' brùthadh nan caorach,
guthan àrd ag èigheachd
's a' gearain, 's a' gàireachdainn
's gach druim thugams'
gam ghlasadh a-mach.

Mi seasamh, 's a' coimhead
's a' feitheamh airson facal
mo ghluasad gu feum.

Mi siubhal gu slaodach
a' cruinneachadh nan uan
's gan ruagadh romham
a-steach gu càch;
uain a' ruith
gu meulaich màth'r.
Boinneagan uisge
mar mhillean mialan
a' leum às an dup,
agus crathadh cinn nan adharcan
fliuch, fuar, feagalach
a' dèanamh às.

Ceum no dhà eile
's chì mi aodannan nan gàir'.
Mo làmhan fhìn a' breith air clòimh,
fàileadh an dup air mo chorragan,
peant a' comharradh mo chasan,
poll dubh bog air mo bhòtannan
's mo chànan fhìn nam bheul.

At the Fank

Standing over by the prairie gate
with clean grass under my wellies,
cold hands in my pockets,
the smell of the sheep dip
faintly
hesitantly
coming to my nostrils
as I watch the others gathered
around the fank
and laughing with each other:
pushing the sheep,
loud voices shouting
and moaning, and laughing
and all with their backs to me
shutting me out.

I stand, and watch
and wait for a word
to move me to usefulness.

Moving slowly
gathering the lambs
and driving them before me
in towards the others;
lambs running
to a mother's bleat.
Drops of water
jump from the sheep dip
like millions of fleas
and the horns' head-shaking,
wet, cold, fearful
running off.

Another step or two
and I can see the laughing faces.
My own hands holding wool,
the smell of sheep dip on my fingers.
Paint marking my legs,
soft black mud on my wellies
and my own language on my tongue.

ACKNOWLEDGEMENTS

Thanks are due to the following copyright holders for permission to publish the poems in this anthology:

Carol Ann Duffy 'The captain of the 1964 *Top of the Form* Team' is from *Mean Time*, published in 1993 by Anvil Press Poetry. 'Translating the English, 1989', 'Originally', 'The Way My Mother Speaks', 'A shilling for the Sea' and 'Poet for Our Times' are from *The Other Country*, published by Anvil Press Poetry in 1990. 'Mouth, with Soap', 'Politics' and 'Plainsong' are from *Selling Manhattan*, published in 1987 by Anvil Press Poetry. 'Ash Wednesday 1984' and 'The B Movie' are from *Standing Female Nude*, published in 1985 by Anvil Press Poetry.

John Burnside To author and Carcanet Press Ltd for poems from *The Hoop*, © John Burnside, 1988. Secker and Warburg Ltd, and *Verse*

Peter McCarey To author and Broch Books

Alan Riach To author and Auckland University Press

Elizabeth Burns To author and Polygon

William Hershaw To author and Mercat Press

Robert Alan Jamieson To author and Polygon

Robert Crawford To author, Polygon and Chatto and Windus for poems from *Scottish Assembly*, © Robert Crawford, 1990.

David Kinloch To author and Vennel Press

Meg Bateman To author and *Verse*

Iain Bamforth To author and Carcanet Press Ltd for poems from *Sons and Pioneers*, © Iain Bamforth, 1992.

Graham Fulton To author and Polygon

Daniel O'Rourke To author, Vennel Press and *Verse*

Maud Sulter To author and Urban Fox

Jackie Kay To author and Bloodaxe Books Ltd. From *The Adoption Papers*, © Jackie Kay, 1991.

W.N. Herbert To author, Galliard, Vennel Press and Polygon

Kathleen Jamie To author, Bloodaxe Books Ltd, *Times Literary Supplement* 'Things which shall never be', 'The Way We Live' and 'Permanent Cabaret' are from *The Way We Live* © Kathleen Jamie 1987 (Bloodaxe Books Ltd). 'Xiahe' is from *The Autonomous Region: Poems and Photographs from Tibet* by Kathleen Jamie and Sean Mayne Smith (Bloodaxe Books, 1993).

Don Paterson To author and Faber and Faber Ltd Poems from *Nil Nil* © Don Paterson, 1993.

Raymond Friel To author and Southfields Press

Angela McSeveney To author and Polygon

Richard Price To author and Vennel Press

Roddy Lumsden To author, *Verse* and Faber and Faber Ltd

Stuart A. Paterson To author, *Verse*, *Chapman*, *Spectrum*

Alison Kermack To author and Clocktower Press

Anne Frater To author and Polygon